Please read ;
be glad y[...]
As a Christian I
left the negative
but knew the
positive ,

The
Separation
Illusion

" World crisis "
from Illinois. Henry Clay Warmoth
said If he became mayor
of Louisiana just after the
Civil war he would invent
a machine that would
pump the blood from the
black man's veins and replace
it with the blood of a white
man. At the close of the civil
war totalitarian efforts were evident
mostly black men were put in
Washington's Government but no
white man in Virginia was
allowed to represent his state
in the Senate

The Separation Illusion

A Lawyer Examines
the First Amendment

John W. Whitehead

BOX 236, MILFORD, MI. 48042

Printed in the United States of America

Library of Congress Cataloging in Publication Data

Whitehead, John W 1946-
   The separation illusion.
   Bibliography:
   Includes index.
1. Church and state in the United States—History. 2. Christianity—
United States. 3. United States—Moral conditions. I. Title.
BR516.W447   261.7'0973   77-7045
ISBN 0-915134-41-1 pbk.

To

My Father and Mother

Contents

Foreword

Those who disagree with John Whitehead's study have no trouble in understanding it. After all, they have been busy for some time in working to create a country radically different from the intentions of the Founding Fathers. It is, unfortunately, in the ranks of those who should be on Attorney Whitehead's side that the confusion exists, and many evangelical leaders are insistent that the idea that a Christian America ever existed is a myth.

To cite a very specific example, although the Dutch community in the United States is an exceptionally strong, stable, patriotic, and conservative element, a large segment of its clergy has almost a pathological hatred of the United States and is insistent that it has never been Christian. I have myself had the experience of seeing such theologians and pastors get up and leave a meeting in dissent when I spoke favorably of America's Christian heritage!

Why is this so? There are two reasons for it, apart from ignorance. First, we live in an age of paper religion. We believe more in issuing paper pronouncements on all subjects than in living our faith. The paper pronouncements of America's once Christian establishment are not many. Hence, it is assumed that the United States was never Christian.

Second, most religious leaders still have an Old World church and state perspective. If the United States was ever Christian, the Constitution would have said so, they believe. But because it said nothing, it believed nothing. The faith of the early Republic, however, was hostile to the establishment of a church from above, or religious controls from above. The idea was to create a situation in which Christianity would be the established faith from the ground level and free to prosper accordingly. The purpose thus of the Constitution was not to express Christian faith but to allow such faith freedom from the state in order to dominate society, law, and education.

Harold O. J. Brown, in *The Reconstruction of the Republic* (1977), has stated this very well:

> *The United States Constitution is not a source of fundamental values. It is an instrument whereby fundamental values can be protected, defining the procedures, principles, and methods whereby government can function to allow the people to give content to their lives. But the Constitution itself cannot give that content.* [P. 19]

In the Old World, the state gives that content: it makes itself the source of fundamental values. In the United States, *at the insistence of the clergy,* the Constitution omitted all such definitions: they were to come from the grace of God, operative in society, not from the grace of the state.

Our problem today is that both non-Christians and Christians are trying to view the Constitution and the United States in terms of Old World categories. They are assuming that a definition of fundamental values is present in the Constitution by virtue of the absence of Christian declarations. As a result, they are distorting our law, our country, and our history.

John Whitehead, as a careful and able lawyer, recalls us to the basic legal facts. His study thus deserves careful and widespread attention.

ROUSAS JOHN RUSHDOONY

July 1977
Vallecito, CA

Acknowledgments

The author would like to take this opportunity to offer the deepest words of thanks and appreciation to the Reverend Rousas John Rushdoony for his sound advice, unwavering support, and vast knowledge in addition to the unlimited use of his expansive library. I would like, further, to thank John Weldon, the author of several publications, who gave me every encouragement and aid during the researching and writing of this book. A personal word of gratitude is due my wife, Carolyn, for her invaluable typing and editing of the manuscript, and my son, Jayson, for his patience and his unselfish sacrifice of many outings that this book might be written.

Introduction

Benjamin Franklin once remarked, "If men are so wicked as we now see them with religion, what would they be without it." Franklin lived at a time when the accepted foundation of truth was the holy Scriptures. He had also participated in the American War of Independence which established the greatest Christian nation this world has ever known.

Even though Franklin wasn't a Christian himself, he knew that once his fellow countrymen forsook the absolute truths of the Bible the only result would be trouble for the nation. He had enough perspective to realize that all men need some sort of bounds within which to work. If not, man becomes a law unto himself, and this in turn leads to violent lawlessness.

Proverbs 28:12 instructs us: "When the righteous triumph there is great glory, but when the wicked rise, men hide themselves."* Forsaking the Scriptures as a guide for all things leads not only to chaos but also, as history has illustrated, to the totalitarian state—a government that totally controls its citizens. This type of state is necessary when man runs rampant, for he must be restrained. In the process man has been enslaved and tortured, and as a result eventually destroyed.

Digging the Pit

The question has been asked: If the United States was once so prosperous with Christianity as its foundation, then why have the people forsaken the Christian way to follow the dark path that is eating away at present-day America? The answer to this question is the object of this book. The cause of modern man's dilemma is

---

*All Scripture references are from the New American Standard Bible unless otherwise noted.

what I have called *The Separation Illusion.* Whenever man abandons the true God while attempting to build a utopia (or what has been called the "Great Society") apart from the Creator he only succeeds in digging himself into a pit—a pit of no return.

Brave New World?

Modern man has promulgated the view that he can go his own way without assistance from God. Why has this happened?

This problem is analyzed by looking first at the institutional church because the church is to be a salt or preservative in any culture. The contemporary church appears largely to have forgotten Christ's command to go and make disciples of all nations (Matthew 28:19). A society or culture stands or falls by the way the Christian community relates truth to the people. Why the church has been ineffective in its duty to man is the focus of the first chapter.

In the next chapter, entitled "Post-America," the idea is presented that we live not only in a post-Christian culture but also in a post-American culture. The country established by the Founding Fathers was something totally different from what is now referred to as America.

"The Shift" is an analysis of how the American governmental system has changed from a group of tightly knit states to a highly centralized phenomenon. The government in Washington was once a relatively isolated institution, but it now seems to have acquired an octopuslike function as its tentacles reach into the most private sectors of our lives.

In the next three chapters the pervasive idea that there is a "wall of separation" between church and state is placed under the microscope. Thomas Jefferson was the originator of the wall-of-separation phrase, which has been utilized by the United States Supreme Court to disestablish the Christian church and to remove its influence in the schools and thus on all youth. As is shown, the Constitution erects no wall between church and state, but, instead, exposes the fact that the famous wall of separation is an illusion. The prayer and the Bible-reading decisions of the Court illustrate our move from "One Nation Under God" to "One Nation Under the Supreme Court."

The chapter called "Valley of the Bones" illustrates that the separation illusion is destroying American youth, both Christian and non-Christian. The horror is presented that a youth fuehrer is being sought by the young, and the possibilities of a tyrannical youth are discussed.

In the two concluding chapters the reader is given a glimpse of the coming "brave new world" in which there is only an illusion of freedom, nothing more. The picture presented is not a pretty one, but the hope is that a Christian reformation will turn the tide.

A. D. One

This is not a book of utter despair. It is a book meant to inform the reader that action can be taken to prevent the present decay of our nation from spreading any further.

The true hope, as emphasized, is the return to the holy Scriptures as man's guide. It is necessary that man seek answers in God's revelation instead of looking to politicians and psychiatrists for solutions to what in actuality are spiritual problems. The answer was given to man two thousand years ago at the cross. Christ, and only Christ, provides the answer to modern man's dilemma. Until man recognizes this, the separation illusion will continue to plague him.

Prologue

In recent years Christians and non-Christians alike have been questioning whether America was ever a Christian nation. Without doubt it was, but secular historians have eradicated as much Christian influence as possible from history. While they profess to write history objectively, it is a fact that no man is objective about religion. Since all men are made in the image of God, all men thereby are religious, whether it is the Christian religion or the religion of secular humanism that they profess.

A Christian Nation?

In 1892 the United States Supreme Court made an exhaustive study of the supposed connection between Christianity and the government of the United States. After reviewing hundreds of volumes of historical documents, the Court asserted, "These references ... add a volume of unofficial declarations to the mass of organic utterances that this is a religious people ... a Christian nation."[1] Likewise, in 1931 Supreme Court Justice George Sutherland reviewed the 1892 decision in reference to another case and reiterated that Americans are a "Christian people."[2] And in 1952 Justice William O. Douglas affirmed that "we are a religious people and our institutions presuppose a Supreme Being."[3]

In the 1740s, when it seemed that perhaps Christian influence was dwindling, the Great Awakening swept America. During this period evangelicals united as never before. Mass outpourings of emotion bordered on hysteria as people wept and rolled on the ground. Churches of all Protestant denominations, except the Anglicans, received thousands of new members.[4] It has been estimated that one-sixth of the population of New England was converted in a two-year period[5] (this fails to recognize the number that was already Christian).

Edwin Gaustad reports that in 1740 there were 1,176 established churches in America.[6] Following the influence of the Great Awakening, by 1780 there were 2,731 established churches for thirteen scantily populated states—well over a 100 percent increase![7]

When the Constitution was adopted and sent to the states for ratification, the population of America numbered only about three and one-half million. The Christian population, however, numbered at least two million. James C. Hefley has commented that about "900,000 were Scotch or Scotch–Irish Presbyterians, with another million also holding to basic Calvinistic beliefs."[8]

Up to the time of the drafting of the Constitution and beyond, state laws forbade anyone from holding office unless he was a Christian. Moreover, as late as 1864 the Maryland Constitution required that a citizen desiring a public office must have declared "belief in the Christian religion, or of the existence of God, and in a future state of rewards and punishments." In New Hampshire a requirement that senators and representatives should be of the "Protestant religion" remained in force until 1877.

In most states there were religious requirements for citizenship and voting, religious oaths, laws prohibiting blasphemy, laws requiring a trinitarian faith, or a firm belief in the infallibility of Scripture, and laws barring non-Christians as witnesses in court.[9] There were also in many states laws that called for imprisonment of anyone who was an atheist. A writer named Warren Chase recorded that in the 1820s "an old man was imprisoned sixty days in Boston for publishing in his own paper the fact that he didn't believe in their orthodox God."[10]

The laws up to and after ratification of the Constitution were premised on the fact that the respective states were Christian, and anti-Christianity constituted treasonable activity or belief.[11] Since the basic foundation of the government was Christian, it had to be protected legally.

It doesn't take a great deal of insight to conclude that the majority of the people in the United States at the time of the drafting of the Constitution were Christian. The rest of the non-Christian population lived under laws that were either written directly from the Scriptures or influenced by them. The common presuppositional base of that day was clearly taken from the Christian Bible.

A Clockwork Orange?

The argument has been raised that deism played a very large role in the founding of America. It has also been said that the early fathers were, as a collective, deists. This is an erroneous assumption that has been fostered by many non-Christian historians, not the least of whom is Richard B. Morris, in *Seven Who Shaped America*. Such assumptions deny the early Christian character of our country.

Deism is the belief that God has, much like a clockmaker a clock, made and wound the universe and then abandoned it to its own workings.[12] In other words, the world is a machine and it will keep on ticking and ticking. Deism presents us with an impersonal God who never works in history or the affairs of men.[13] The deist has no need to pray because God, the absentee landlord, is not listening anyway.

In its essence deism denies the deity of Christ and the existence of the Christian Trinity. It also denies the doctrine of original sin, holding that man is good and that he can perfect himself.

Christianity holds that man is a depraved sinner who can gain salvation (what a deist would call perfection) only through regeneration provided by Christ at the cross. Christianity and deism, therefore, do not complement one another but are diametrical opposites.

It is not to be denied that there were deistic influences that played a part in the American Revolution. But were the Founding Fathers deists?

The two men among the early fathers who are most cited as being deists are Thomas Jefferson and Benjamin Franklin. However, neither of these men fits the definition of a deist. From their statements it would seem that they at least believed in the personal God of the Scriptures even if they denied the deity of Christ.

Witness, for example, a plea for public prayer made by Franklin on June 28, 1787, at the Constitutional Convention. Dissension had developed in the convention, and Franklin offered a solution:

We have not hitherto once thought of humbly applying to the Father of Lights to illuminate our understanding. In the beginning of the contest with Great Britain, when we

*were sensible to danger, we had daily prayers in this room
for divine protection.*

*Our prayers, sir, were heard, and they were gra-
ciously answered ... do we imagine that we no longer need
His assistance? I have lived, sir, a long time, and the
longer I live, the more convincing proofs I see of this
truth—that God governs the affairs of men.*

*And if a sparrow cannot fall to the ground without
His notice, is it probable an empire can rise without His
aid? We have been assured, sir, in the sacred writings that
except the Lord build the house, they labor in vain that
build it. . . . I firmly believe this. . . .*

Franklin then asked that prayers be held each morning before pro-
ceeding with business in Congress. This resolution passed, and the
practice of having prayer before the daily sessions of the United
States Congress continues to this day.

Benjamin Franklin's remarks are clearly derived from the holy
Scriptures revealing that very likely he was operating from Christian presuppositions himself. Moreover, it is obvious that Franklin
made an appeal for prayer based on the Scriptures because he was
speaking to a group of men in Congress who were predominantly
Christian.

In George Whitefield's later years this fine evangelist of the
Great Awakening had a strong influence over Franklin[14] (he was 83
when he offered the prayer before Congress). When Whitefield was
denied church pulpits during the Great Awakening, Benjamin
Franklin and other admirers constructed a building to accommodate the great crowds who wished to hear the English evangelist.[15]
Later, in 1751, Franklin and his associates opened an academy in
that very building, which forty years later became the University of
Pennsylvania. A life-sized statue of Whitefield stands today in one
of the quadrangles of the university.

It is interesting to note the high opinion Franklin had of the
Christian religion. No knowledge, he wrote, is more important than
"that of being a good parent, a good child, a good husband or wife,
a good neighbor or friend, a good subject or citizen, that is, in
short, a good Christian."[16] Franklin also said that history should be
presented to show the excellence of the Christian religion above all
others.

Thomas Jefferson shared a very similar view. Consider his earnest words:

> Can the liberties of a nation be sure when we remove their only firm basis, a conviction in the minds of the people, that these liberties are the gift of God? That they are not to be violated but with His wrath? Indeed, I tremble for my country, when I reflect that God is just; that His justice cannot sleep forever, that revolution of the wheel of fortune, a change of situation, is among possible events; that it may become probable by supernatural influence! The Almighty has no attribute which can take side with us in that event.[17]

Although both Franklin and Jefferson were influenced by deism (among other things), unless one charges that both were hypocrites, it is equally clear that they were not deists. In plain and forthright language these two men set forth Calvinism's doctrines of predestination and total providence while including a Unitarian view of the subordination of Christ's person in the Godhead.[18] Moreover, God is seen by these men not as an absentee clockmaker but as someone to appeal to and be fearful of. Though no easy classification can be made of their faith, to call Franklin and Jefferson true deists is as erroneous as to call Karl Barth an evangelical Christian.

Deism and the Masses

During the years of the American Revolution when deism had its strongest influence, it was confined to a small elite. The deists frowned upon dissemination of their views because they believed Christianity, since it had such a widespread effect, was beneficial to the so-called masses (especially since the Christian religion had preserved the good order of the country).[19] Therefore, the great bulk of the people inhabiting the United States between 1740 (the height of the Great Awakening) and 1789 (the year the Constitution was ratified) were either Christian or living lives based on Christian presuppositions.

The Christian character of the country was yet intact in the early 1800s and was so attested by the notable French historian

Alexis de Tocqueville in his treatise *Democracy in America*.[20] As mentioned above, even after the Revolution most of the colonies restricted voting and the holding of public office to Christians.[21] Again, the Christian nature of America pushes aside the myth that deism was the controlling factor in early America.

The Eleven-Year Itch

The American War for Independence produced a clamor that drowned out to some degree the Puritan influence that had predominated in colonial America. The Christian voice returned in the early 1780s, but these in-between years produced a host of confusion on our continent. It wasn't until the Christian influence was written into the Constitution in 1787 that the disorientation subsided.

In 1781 the United States was governed by a curious document called the Articles of Confederation. Influenced by Jeffersonian philosophy, the Articles formed an extremely weak federal government. Congress had no power to levy taxes, and within a few years the government was on the verge of bankruptcy. A call went out to revise this document.

The radical or agrarian, antifederalist philosophy that had prevailed in the Articles of Confederation caused the colonies to question their earlier leadership. As a result, only eight of the fifty-six signers of the Declaration of Independence were present at the Constitutional Convention[22] (not all the people who had adhered to Jefferson's philosophy were aware of the implications of his thinking).[23] Instead, the Christian view of government—that government is necessary to check the sinful propensities in men—was now emerging with a new vigor, and by 1787 Christianity had again gained popular support.[24] Many now saw the new Constitution as a remedy for the ills of the day which they attributed to the radicalism of Jefferson and his following.

There is little doubt that the membership at the Philadelphia Constitutional Convention in 1787 was more attuned to the Christian world view.[25] C. Gregg Singer comments on the absence of the radical element at the framing of the Constitution in Philadelphia:

> *Of greater significance is the fact that very few of the radicals of 1776 found their way into the Philadelphia meet-*

ing. Franklin was there, to be sure, but a subdued Franklin in contrast to the philosopher of 1776. Conspicuous for their absence were the most forceful of the liberal deist leaders: Jefferson, Richard Henry Lee, and Thomas Paine. There is abundant evidence that evangelical Christianity was held in much higher respect by the majority in the Convention of 1787 than it had been in 1776.... The Christian world and life view was accorded greater weight by the delegates than ... in ... 1776 ... they were willing to accept the benefits of the Gospel in the political and social life of the American people.... The Convention of 1787 displayed a consciousness of the meaning of the doctrine of sin ... it is conceded that a ... Christian philosophy permeated the thinking and actions of the members.[26]

There can be no comparison of the Declaration and Articles with the Constitution. By the time of the writing of the Constitution, deism and other philosophies had faded and been replaced by the sanity and reasonableness of Christianity. Some church historians have gone so far as to suggest that Calvinism was written directly into the Constitution.[27] In fact, the checks and balances system and the doctrine of enumerated powers found in the Constitution attest to the Christian belief that man is depraved, and in order to ensure that no one man or group should attain too much power, the federal government was limited to express powers only. The truth, as John Warwick Montgomery says, is that "17th-century Christian principles of limited government were directly incorporated into our Constitution, providing appropriate checks and balances on human sinfulness."[28]

It is also evident that the biblical concept of the covenant as interpreted by John Calvin is implicit in the preamble of the Constitution. "We the people of the United States" harks back to the Mayflower Compact (drafted by Calvinistic Puritans), which began, "We whose names are underwritten." The Pilgrim covenant can be traced through Calvin to God's agreement with Israel: "If ye will obey my voice ... and keep my covenant, then ye shall be a peculiar treasure unto me" (Exodus 19:5; King James Version).

The concept of a secular state was nonexistent in 1776 as well as 1787, and no less so in 1791 when the Bill of Rights was adopted.

Rousas John Rushdoony is on target when he comments: "To read the Constitution as the charter for a secular state is to misread history, and to misread it radically. The Constitution was designed to perpetuate a Christian order."[29]

Why then was there any absence of reference specifically to Christianity in the Constitution? "The response must be equally blunt: There is an absence of reference because the framers of the Constitution did not believe that this was an area of jurisdiction for the federal government. It would not have occurred to them to attempt to re-establish that which the colonists had fought against, namely, religious control and establishment by the central government. . . . This was an area of states' rights, not federal control."[30] In other words, the Constitution is founded on the principle of enumerated powers. This means that the federal government has only that power which it is granted in the Constitution. Since Christianity was not mentioned in the Constitution, the federal government had no control over it.

Singer concludes: "Christian theism had so permeated the colonial mind that it continued to *guide* even those who had come to regard the Gospel with indifference or even hostility."[31] The eleven-year itch of disorganization was scratched by Christian and non-Christian men who were guided by biblical presuppositions. Non-Christian historians have on the whole attempted with great success to erase the Christian influence from the Constitution. Careful study not only uncovers a Christian influence on this document but also reveals that Christianity and the holy Scriptures were the guiding lights in its drafting.

Although the Constitution was not a religious creed and Christ was not mentioned, its principles were drawn from the thoughts of men who knew and understood the Scriptures. The Constitution was, as historian H. G. Wells declared, "indubitably Christian."

﹛ 1 ﹜

The Separation Illusion

We were talking about the space between us all,
And the people who hide themselves behind a wall of
  illusion,
Never glimpse the truth;
Then it's far too late when they pass away.

George Harrison

Futility of futilities! All is futile.

King Solomon
Ecclesiastes 1:2

In the 1960s when screaming young girls were down on their knees before the Beatles in concert, as if in prayer, there was little condemnation coming from Christianity. John Lennon, one of the Beatles, broke the silence in 1966 when he casually remarked, "Christianity will go. It will vanish and shrink. I needn't argue about that. I'm right, and I will be proved right. We're more popular than Jesus Christ now. I don't know which will go first. Rock 'n' roll or Christianity. Jesus was alright, but his disciples were thick and ordinary. It's them twisting it that ruins it for me."[1]

The four cute lads from Liverpool were no longer "little boys." Now they were ugly old men who had prophesied the death of Christianity with the assertion that they were more popular than God Himself. The deceptive illusion that so many had labored under so long, namely, that Christianity could be reconciled with something as worldly as the Beatles, came crashing down.

Richard Pritchard of Westminster Presbyterian Church in Madison, Wisconsin, said that anyone outraged by Lennon's statement should blame himself and not the Beatles. Such people should, he said, "take a look at their own values and standards. There is much validity in what Lennon said. To many people the golf course is also more popular than Jesus Christ."[2]

Lennon publicly retracted his statement by admitting, "I'm sorry now I opened my mouth."[3] Subsequently, the *Chicago Daily News* proclaimed, "Lennon Forgiven: Beatles Mosey On, Richer Than Ever."[4] The "Christian nation" of America had slipped back into wishful thinking by forgiving Lennon for his "slip of the tongue."

The Beatles are an example of the illusion that we all live in from time to time. We wish for things to be a certain way when we know they never can be. Even many Christians believe that somehow certain areas of life can be separated from God. The non-Christian believes he can separate his total existence from God.

The God of the Scriptures has said, however, that "the world is mine, and all it contains" (Psalm 50:12). The "all" includes every man, every government, and every church. There is nothing separate from God. The Lord utilizes even the non-Christian for His purposes. For instance, Balaam and his talking ass served God's plan very well.

The separation illusion has the modern world in its crushing grasp. It takes a full-orbed Christian outlook, however, to understand that we are His, and that any escape from His sovereignty is impossible.

Freud's Illusion

Modern man has fallen prey to the same temptation that Eve succumbed to in the Garden of Eden. It is the desire to "be like God," having the capacity to determine the difference between good and evil (Genesis 3:5). Once man accepts the philosophy that he can determine for himself, without utilizing God's revelation, the difference between good and evil, he starts believing he is autonomous from God. Man now, like a god, is separate and can work on his own to effectuate his purposes. Man can now proclaim with Nietzsche, "Dead are all Gods; now we desire the superman

to live." The Christian religion is thus suspect for it allows no
supermen within its doctrines. It is a stranger in a world of human
gods.

Sigmund Freud, a superman alive and a deity dead, vented his
hatred of religion in most of his works. In *The Future of an Illusion*
he hurls semantic missiles not only at the Christian religion but at
God Himself.

Freud wrote basically in religious terms with an apparent
familiarity with Christian theology. He radically differed with
Christian theology, however, in dissociating *guilt* from *sin*. He recognized guilt as man's basic problem. Why? Through
psychoanalysis (primarily of himself) Freud discovered three dark
horrors written in man's primitive past—incest, parricide, and
cannibalism. He developed the idea of the "primal horde" as one
of the bases of his theory. The "violent primal father" drove out
the sons and thereafter claimed exclusive sexual possession of the
mother and daughters.[5] Each of the brothers hated and feared the
father. Finally, the rebellious sons joined together and ate the
father, thereby gaining possession of the mother and sisters.

After the boys had satisfied their hate of the primitive father,
they discovered that they also loved him. Guilt overcame them.
Each brother wanted the mother and daughters to himself, and instead of fighting to the death the brothers erected the taboo of *incest*. The dead father was now stronger than when he was alive.

From all this hocus-pocus originated the three basic instincts
of man—*incest* (primarily, sexual relations with close relatives),
parricide (murder of the parents) and *cannibalism* (basically, the
desire to eat the father). According to Freudian theory, in every
modern man these instincts yet exist, thereby causing one to desire
sexual intercourse with his mother and also to desire to kill and eat
his father.

It was the relationship with the father, however, that literally
gave man fits. As a child he stood helpless before the towering
figure of the father. Freud theorized that the father also constituted
a danger to the child, possibly because of its earlier relation to the
mother. The child is caught in a vise, for he loves the father while
hating him. As the child grows older and moves away from his
father, he longs for him. This is a crucial phase in the development
of religion.

Freud states, "The primal father was the original image of God, the model on which later generations have shaped the figure of God."[6] As man stands helpless before the natural world, he longs for a protector. Man has therefore created the illusion of God the Father. The need for God is thus an illusion created to fill the vacancy left by the departed father. To Freud the belief in God was the result of an illusionary obsessional neurosis. Amazingly enough, his theories form the basis of most modern psychiatric thought.

Freud shot forth his propaganda with little regard for the consequences. He saw man as an enemy of civilization because every man seeks to express his instincts to kill and rape. Although he expressed the belief that religion with its "lording-over" approach kept instinctually primitive man somewhat in line, it had to go or civilization would run the risk of basking in illusion.

In his book *Moses and Monotheism* Freud proclaimed himself the murderer of Moses and a new messiah. He would "save" man from his guilt. How? By psychoanalysis. "Psychoanalysis is my creation," he said. Its result, of course, leads to "a denial of God and of a moral idea."[7] Through psychoanalysis Freud had shown that there was no God to be found in man's soul. Freud believed that God must be removed from autonomous man at all costs.

Science and Reason, what he called *Logos,* were his god. Science, he stated, had reduced man to the common brute and Darwin had taken away the one thing that placed man above the beasts— special creation. Copernicus robbed man of the idea that the earth was the center of the universe. Man was now a speck among specks.

Why did Freud go to such pains to destroy any inkling of God or religion? When the Light shines on their dark deeds, men hide. They erect lies and illusions as forms of escape.

Freud himself defined *illusion* as basically "wishful thinking." An illusion is not the same thing as error. For example, Aristotle's belief that vermin are developed out of dung is an error, not an illusion. As Freud points out, it was an illusion of Columbus that he had discovered a new sea route to the Indies. Illusions are derived from "human wishes."[8]

It is wishful thinking for man to believe that he can truly become autonomous from the Creator. Rather than bow before God, man erects a wall of illusion between himself and his Lord. Ignoring Him, however, will not make Him go away.

The Freudian Church

Beatle John Lennon struck the chords of truth when he intimated that Christianity was dying. To most non-Christians, it must appear that it is only a matter of time before the church gags on the pollution of compromise.

Sigmund Freud asserted throughout his writings that psychoanalysis was leading to the denial of religion and, therefore, a denial of God. In apparent agreement, the neurotic modern world has become so "Freudian" in its viewpoint that there is very little room for God.

Freud recognized his role all too clearly. He saw himself as a type of Satan and as a deliverer of mankind—a messiah. Freud declared, "Do you know that I am the Devil? All my life I have had to play the Devil, in order that others would be able to build the most beautiful cathedral with the materials that I produced."[9]

Psychoanalysis, like the big bad wolf, has huffed and puffed and has almost blown the house down. But genuine Christianity can no more be reconciled with psychoanalysis than with Marxism, or with any other anti-God philosophy.

With its emphasis on self-probing to seek answers to life's dilemmas, psychoanalysis has been an important factor in the change of approach taken by the modern church in its attempts to spread the good news. The Christian church, which once viewed the Christian life as a tree that should produce fruit, is now looking at the roots, or inner being of the individual. This is Freudian psychoanalysis—the same tool that Freud utilized to drive God from the soul.

When the Christian is looking at his roots he is looking at Jesus Christ, for Christ is the root of the Christian life (Colossians 2:7). The Christian seeks Him through prayer, not through psychoanalysis. Jesus Christ through the Holy Spirit manifests the fruits, works, and accomplishments that should be apparent in the true Christian. As Christ said in the Sermon on the Mount, "You will know them by their fruits" (Matthew 7:16). The emphasis is on external manifestation, not internal anxiety.

With the acceptance of the psychoanalytic approach by the church, it is little wonder that many Christians are caught up in their own problems. One who is lost in himself is helpless to do much about the world around him. The great battle, however, is raging outside the walls of the church. Out there in the thick of it is where the Christian church needs to confront the culture with the truth of Jesus Christ. But the salt for decades has been entombed within the institutional church while the American society is decaying. Jesus' apostles confronted the world. The modern church is planning its next board meeting.

The problem within Christendom is not psychological but indeed theological. The Christian should judge himself according to the only true standard—God's Word. But too many Christians have been assessing themselves according to a fallible and subjective standard—self-analysis through inner probing. In the process, the church has developed an existential, experience-oriented mentality.

With the healing and assurance of salvation the Christian can rely rather on the Scriptures to eliminate anxiety than on psychoanalysis. Psychology, like any other pseudoreligion, when mixed with Christianity, parasitically extracts its vital energy. To change the figure, psychology, like quicksand, will swallow the church if Christianity does not return to the true source of knowledge.

The United States was once a Christian nation. The church has stepped back much too long. It has literally let down not only God but also the American people by failing to keep the faith intact. Assisting the church's retreat is the separation illusion, which is draining Christianity of its vitality. God created man to act and to rule (Genesis 1:27, 28), not to hide within the institutional church. Likewise, the secular world is hiding in its homes with chains on its doors. Let Christians come out and be separate.

The Liberated Church

Long tolerant of communism in its various Stalinist, Titoesque, and Maoist guises, many churchmen have openly endorsed revolution. A congressional investigator found that 7,000 clergymen once espoused the Communist party line. Some have now veered off to more popular forms of Marxism.[10]

A London conference that was organized by the World Council of Churches produced a report which declared that "guerrilla fighters struggling against racist regimes must be given the support of the church if all else has been seen to fail."[11] Under the chairmanship of Senator George McGovern, a Methodist lay delegate, the conference said that in certain circumstances, "The church must support resistance movements, including revolutions, which are aimed at the elimination of political or economic tyranny that makes racism possible."[12]

Churchmen have avowed support to civil disobedience. Many have been jailed for unlawful picketing.[13] A prime example is Yale University chaplain William Sloane Coffin, Jr., who, along with Dr. Benjamin Spock, gained fame for his resistance to the Vietnam War.

This type of activity is a result of denying the validity of the Scriptures, thereby "freeing" man to be autonomous from God's revelation. The separation illusion is clearly perpetrated by denying clear Scriptural instruction against civil disobedience as found in Romans 13. Revolution and civil disobedience are not the means that will effect a change in government. The key to change is *regeneration* because it is not the government that is bad but the unregenerate man in the government that pollutes the system.

For the most part, the church has clearly compromised the biblical message of regeneration in order to be appealing to an ungodly culture. Atheist B. F. Skinner relates this change to behaviorism. The new approach to child rearing is to reward the child for good behavior instead of punishing him for bad.[14] Religious agencies, following the trend, have moved from a threat of hell-fire to an overemphasis on God's love.[15]

The Christian faith has been "separated" not only from the state (or government) but, so it seems in many instances, from the institutionalized church as well. When this occurs, judgment is sure to follow.

The Laughing Church

Theologian Reinhold Niebuhr once wrote, "Humor is, in fact, a prelude to faith; and laughter is the beginning of prayer." The ability to laugh at oneself is the first essential step to prayer for repentance and forgiveness, he asserted. Niebuhr cautioned, however, that even laughter has its limits: "Laughter, when pressed to solve the ultimate issue, turns into a vehicle of bitterness rather than joy. To laugh at life in the ultimate sense means to scorn it."

Contemporary Christians are beginning to take Niebuhr's philosophy seriously. A story in the *Los Angeles Times* entitled "Laughter in Churches" reported that at a recent religious education conference two thousand Catholics attended four "laughter workshops," while an additional sixteen hundred attended a weekend session on "When Jesus Laughed."[16] Accompanying the article is a photograph that depicts a dozen churchmen standing before an altar guffawing, with their hands on their midsections.[17]

In the same newspaper story Jesus Christ is depicted as the clown prince of all times. Taking its cue from an article in the *Christian Century* magazine, the story commented, "The lowly birth in a donkey shed of a man-savior later hailed by generations is typical of the stock of clowns."[18]

As also reported, the Reverend Floyd Shaffer found that dressing up as a clown and doing a pantomime near the pulpit has livened up his Sunday night services.[19] Said the Reverend Mr. Shaffer, "Dignity can degenerate to dullness."[20]

The Reverend Matthew Fox, author of two books, one entitled *Whee! We, Wee All the Way Home: Toward a Sensual Spirituality,* pleads that Christians need to seek pleasure and be more "sensual."[21] After proclaiming his "good sensual news" in Texas recently, Fox said a nun came up to him and remarked, "Father, listening to you talk makes me feel a little naughty."[22] Reverend Mr. Fox, being the perceptive man he is, replied, "Sister, if you heard Jesus, you'd do better than that. You'd feel dirty."[23]

Seeming to take Fox's advice literally, the First Unitarian Church of Richardson, Texas, had an exotic stripper dance for the congregation. When "she was through there was nothing left but her G-string and the congregation's imagination."[24] According to Reverend Bill Nichols, "I haven't had a complaint."[25] When asked if she thought her nude dance sparked any feelings other than spiritual, the stripper said, "I don't know what you mean by spiritual. I don't dance to frustrate people. I create a fantasy. I like to turn people on. I really felt good."[26] Nichols likewise remarked on the question, "I don't think anyone was sexually aroused, but I don't consider the erotic aspect of the dance wrong."[27]

The illusion that man can determine for himself what is good and what is evil will eventually enslave man. The good truth is found in the Bible, and it is the pure, clean truth. The Christian cannot sidestep Scripture without distorting his total world view. If Jesus makes one feel dirty then he is dirty indeed, but God is still God and ruler over such a man. He may pretend God isn't there, just as he can pretend that the sun doesn't shine.

"Pop" poet Bob Dylan has summed up modern man's dilemma much better than most:

> Disillusioned words like bullets bark
> As human Gods aim for their mark,
> Made everything from toy guns that spark
> To flesh-colored Christs that glow in the dark.
> It's easy to see without looking too far
> That not much is really sacred.[28]

The Witchdoctors

Following the decline of the Christian religion comes the re-emergence of the witchdoctor, equipped with a bag of cure-alls as old as humanity itself. When the church is strong the shaman, or magical wizard, is forced to work in the shadows. As the light recedes and darkness falls upon the land, he crawls out of his crevice with his black-magic answers. The resurgence of astrology and soothsaying is one clear example of this trend.

The most striking evidence of the decline of religion is the emergence of what some call the "illegitimate branch" of psychology, psychoanalysis. Here in one beguiling package with a pseudoscientific mail-order appeal is nearly all the religious stock-in-trade of ancient man—interpretation of dreams, incest myths, casting out of demons, obsessive sexual teleologies, and confessionals.[29] Sitting atop the totem pole is the grand shaman himself, Sigmund Freud.

In the realm of art and aesthetics, where it has probably done the most harm, psychoanalysis has denigrated man, once thought to be a little lower than the angels, to the level of the brute.[30] The greatest twentieth-century writers in English literature—Eliot, Yeats, and D. H. Lawrence, to name a few—abhorred Sigmund

Freud. Most second-rate writers, however, have made Freudian theory and characters a central part of their works.[31]

Another basis of the modern mentality is man's belief in magic. When man views himself as his own god and creator, total power and control become his goal. By utilizing magic, man attempts to gain such autonomous power and control over the world of man, nature, and the supernatural.[32] By means of this total and autonomous power, "Man expects to govern reality by his own prediction and planning."[33]

Through psychoanalysis man can plan his destiny. He can proclaim the death of God within his soul, and then his life is his to live. Man can reach nirvana here on earth if only he can "work the kinks out." The kinks, however, are caused by a man who believes he can live separate from God and survive. Salvation, not psychoanalysis, is the only answer.

Racial Warfare

What has been written so far has not been an attempt to denigrate Christianity or the church. The purpose has been to highlight what is happening within Christendom today. To say the least, it is nothing to be proud of.

Christianity has compromised repeatedly, to the point that its effectiveness has drastically dwindled. The ultimate cause of the compromise or downfall of any Christian is the result of spiritual warfare. Unfortunately, Christians have been losing this vital confrontation.

The Scriptures divide man into two racial classes—the one in Christ and the other in Adam (I Corinthians 15:22). Christians are the new spiritual race in Christ. Non-Christians are the old race in Adam. The Christians serve God and the non-Christians serve the leader of the ungodly, Satan (John 8:44; I John 3:8-12). Conflict results. It is total spiritual warfare, and is being fought every second of every day (Ephesians 6:10-13). The Christians are indwelt by God Himself, who enables them to overpower spiritual foes. But by unfaith many Christians have rendered themselves powerless.

History instructs man that the more segregated physical races are, the greater is the hostility between them when they are brought together. Thus instructed, the Supreme Court by its 1954 decision in the *Brown* case, which ended segregation in the public schools, sought to reduce tension and conflicts between the races.

This same principle can be applied on the spiritual level. Since the children of God are segregated from the non-Christians, hostility and conflict are generated when the children come into contact with each other. As the races grow apart, lack of understanding develops between them. One side eventually overcomes the other. The stronger side then grows less and less tolerant of the weaker race.

At one time Christians had command of the United States. Through toleration they receded until the non-Christians grew too strong to combat any longer. Once the non-Christians were in power they began eliminating Christianity from the system.

This situation eventually leads to hostility and then to persecution of Christians. Man, being the inherently religious creature he is, seeks atonement for his sins. For example, Richard Nixon, aside from the matter of his own culpability, served as the scapegoat for a sinful nation. In the same way Christians will eventually be persecuted as the hostility toward them quickens.

The only way left to prevent Christianity from being totally polluted in this country is a Christian reformation. This means that the United States as a nation must turn back to God and seek His guidance. This type of revival is not unlikely if the Christian people can avoid the logics of futility.

The Logics of Futility

King Solomon, speaking from the viewpoint of unregenerate man in the book of Ecclesiastes, proclaims that "all is futile." Every attempt by man without God is a futile act destined for destruction.

The trend in modern Christianity seems to assume the same view as unregenerate man. Viewing Christianity as a mere "subculture," the Christian man proclaims, "It is futile to think otherwise."

History proves the modern Christian wrong. Laboring under the illusion that Christianity is and can only be a subculture, he has failed to remember that the United States was once a Christian nation. At the time of the signing of the Declaration of Independence, nine of the thirteen colonies had established churches.[34] The state governments were financially supporting the Christian religion. In most states one had to be a Christian to hold office.

The church eventually gave way to what most historians call "the quest for money" (cf. Matthew 6:24; Luke 16:13). Economically the country began to surge forward, and money became the vogue. The Christian church began to recede, forgetting that when "the good steps back, the evil steps forward."

God, however, has affirmatively spoken against the Christian man who compromises, or recedes before the non-Christian. Proverbs 25:26 (KJV) reads, "A righteous man falling down before the wicked is as a troubled fountain, and a corrupt spring."

Much of the problem in recent years has centered around the Christian's understanding of the basic task that he has been called out to perform. In Genesis 1:28, following His creation of the first man, God instructed Adam to "subdue" or conquer the earth, "and rule ... over every living thing that moves on the earth." There is no indication in Scripture that God's command to Adam that he rule the creation was changed by the Fall. The curse of the Fall simply made it more difficult for man to fulfill the dominion quest.

It essentially boils down to the question of presuppositions. Since this expression will appear throughout the book, it is mandatory that its meaning be understood. A presupposition is the basic idea or theory that one begins with before he examines anything else. Francis Schaeffer defines the word *presupposition* as: "A belief or theory which is assumed before the next step in logic is developed. Such a prior postulate often consciously or unconsciously affects the way a person subsequently reasons."[35]

In other words, if I start with the basic belief or presupposition that God exists and that He is my savior, then everything I consider thereafter will be viewed in light of this basic belief. On the other hand, if I take the attitude that God is dead, then everything takes on a different color.

If I begin with the presupposition that God has commanded me as a Christian man to rule over every aspect of the creation with which I come into contact, and submit it to His lordship, then it makes a world of difference. I can then begin with a seed and before I'm through, if faithful, I can conquer an entire forest. If, on the other hand, the Christian man holds to the presupposition that Christianity is a subculture, then it will always be a subculture. Impotence is the logical conclusion of the subculture reasoning.

Christ's death at the cross redeemed fallen man and made him a new creature. Christ's work substantially healed man, and his work is now blessed if done in subjection to God. Christ at the cross reduced the non-Christian society to a subculture with Satan, the lord of the flies, as its ruler.

The idea of "the Christian subculture" was abhorred by the Puritans. These early Christians crossed the Atlantic Ocean to reach what they called "the Promised Land." In less than a century it was the greatest Christian nation on the earth.

Times have changed, and the government now declares immunity from God's sovereignty. The government believes it can separate itself from the Creator. Romans 13, however, places the government and the church in coterminous positions (neither should dominate the other). They are both ministries of God. The government is to punish the evildoer while protecting the godly in administering God's justice. The government, therefore, as well as the church serves in a *ministerial* position.

With the aid of the United States Supreme Court the American government has said it has no need of the spiritual. It has erected "a wall of separation between church and state." This wall of separation is an illusion, as will be clearly illustrated in subsequent chapters. The Constitution (if at all) separates the institutions but not the faith. The men who drafted the Constitution never dreamed that this country would one day deny the God they honored.

This land can once again be a Christian nation. A reformation is at hand. All that is needed is the dominion-oriented Christian man. God dwells in such. Who, then, can be against the Christian if God is for him?

Theologian Rousas J. Rushdoony in his *Word of Flux* put it well when he said, "The Christians have retreated for over a century into their isolated churches, their holiness meetings, and their endless conferences on prophecy (that invariably warn them of their own impotence in the face of world crises). They have learned, as a successful Volkswagen commercial once put it, to 'think small.' And, to put it bluntly, as a man 'thinketh in his heart, so is he' (Proverbs 23:7)."

Influential behaviorist B. F. Skinner in his bestseller *Beyond Freedom and Dignity* has proposed stripping man of his freedom and worth and placing him in a rigidly controlled state. This reduces man to nothing—zero. Moreover, Skinner doesn't even take time to attack the evangelical church, "probably because he doesn't think it's a threat. Unhappily, he is largely right about this."[36]

If the Christian will not be a conqueror, then he will be conquered. If he will not serve God, then he will be forced to serve fallen man, and, as history informs us, fallen man views all men as disposables.

Christians must translate God's truth into action or face an uncertain future of chaos. Prominent theologians are forecasting a gloomy future for Christianity. For example, the Reverend Martin E. Marty, associate editor of *Christian Century* magazine, states that people may soon begin to take experimental roads with no end, leading to a "different denomination for every three or four people."[37] This is despair. Christianity doesn't have to take this second-best position. Christ died and redeemed the Christian people so they could again be triumphant. As Francis Schaeffer states, "Christians should ... take the *lead* in giving direction to cultural change...."[38]

If the Christian man can change his outlook, he can change the world. It will, however, require an overhauling of present Christian thought. The Christian must act as a preservative of his culture by guiding it. He must stop thinking small and start thinking in terms of the creation mandate to subdue the earth. If he doesn't, we can only recede, and recede again, until there is no place to hide.

₹ 2 ₹

Post-America

> *I have an intellectual inclination for democratic institutions, but I am instinctively an aristocrat, which means that I despise and fear the masses. I passionately love liberty, legality, the respect for rights, but not democracy ... liberty is my foremost passion. That is the truth.*
>
> Alexis de Tocqueville

> *The rise of democracy starts an era of backwardness which will lead nation and state to their death.*
>
> Pierre Joseph Proudhon

The night before that historic landing at Plymouth Rock, the Pilgrims crowded into the tiny hold of their ship to sign the Mayflower Compact. This document was based on biblical principles, and has been labeled by historians the birth certificate of the American Republic.

The Puritans who followed during the great migrations of 1630–1640 established the Massachusetts Bay Colony. In the opening sentence of their New England Confederation they set forth their purpose for crossing the Atlantic Ocean: "We all came into these parts of America with one and the same end, namely, to advance the Kingdom of the Lord Jesus Christ."

It was the ideals of these early Christian Americans that influenced the nation up to the time of the Revolution and beyond. Following the American Revolution, the people of the country were consumed with a zeal to see the nation flourish and grow.

The Times Have Changed

Two hundred years later a different mood prevails throughout the land. From all sides the cry is: "America is dying." Senator Barry Goldwater asked, "What the hell has happened to my America?"[1]

Post-Watergate gloom seems to be clutching the lady of New York Harbor by the throat. Instead of a feeling of celebration for the bicentennial year, a moribund cloud descended on the nation. In the words of Gore Vidal, author of *1876*, there was nothing to celebrate: "I should think a year of mourning would be highly salutary—for our lost innocence, our eroding liberties, our vanishing resources, our ruined environment."[2] Likewise, Goldwater commented, "Economically, morally, materially and otherwise, our country is in the kind of deep trouble that has been known to touch off worldwide depressions and wars."[3]

Beating both Vidal and Goldwater to the punch was yippie Jerry Rubin, who said in the late sixties, "Amerika doesn't have the sniffles or a sore throat: she has a malignant cancer." While Don McLean was singing "Bye, Bye, Miss American Pie," Charles Reich in *The Greening of America* was commenting, "The Constitution and the Bill of Rights have steadily been weakened. The nation has gradually become a rigid managerial hierarchy, with a small elite and a great mass of disenfranchised.... America is one vast, terrifying anticommunity."

The basic problem concerning this country has been overlooked. Though most people realize that we live in a post-Christian culture, few realize that we also live in a post-American culture. America arrived on the *Mayflower,* but it had been dead a long time before that other ship sailed to the moon.

The New Constitution

The Reformation superseded an infallible pope with an infallible Bible. In similar fashion the American Revolution replaced the sway of a king with that of a document. As Thomas Paine wrote in *Common Sense,* "In America the law is king." In 1839 John Quincy Adams remarked, "The Constitution itself had been extorted from the grinding necessity of a reluctant nation."[4]

The committee that framed the Constitution held clandestine meetings and was sworn to secrecy[5] because the members were in the process of changing the structure of the government from a weak confederation of states to a more unified nation. The country had labored under the Articles of Confederation as its governing document close to a decade. It proved, however, to be a document that lacked the authority needed to solidify the nation, and a convention was convened in 1787 to amend the Articles. From the secret committee meetings emerged a new document, which differed significantly from the old Articles.

Following its completion, the Constitution (without a Bill of Rights) was submitted to the state legislatures for ratification. Strong opposition to the Constitution arose. Patrick Henry, a Christian, declared, "I look upon that paper as the most fatal plan that could possibly be conceived to enslave a free people."[6] A significant faction of men such as Patrick Henry, George Mason, and Richard Henry Lee moved to stop ratification if the Constitution was not amended to include a Bill of Rights. In fact, Patrick Henry's long and excellent oratories on the subject were a prime factor in the emergence of the first ten amendments to the Constitution.[7]

The Federalists, who originally opposed the Bill of Rights, agreed to amend the Constitution, believing that if they gave in the new Constitution would have a better chance of being ratified. The states responded to the compromise, and in 1791 the first ten amendments to the Constitution became the Bill of Rights.

Criticism of the Constitution quickly changed to optimistic adoration of the document. It had barely become operative when hostile criticism ceased and gave way to what Woodrow Wilson called "an undiscriminating and almost blind worship of its principles."[8] This worship of the Constitution continued until the Civil War struck a nearly fatal blow to the entire structure of American government.

In the mid-nineteenth century the abolitionists referred to the Constitution as "an agreement with hell," but this shrill heresy only stirred the American people to renew their assertion of the national faith. Even secession by the South was posed as loyalty to the principles of the Constitution and a protest against their violation. In fact, the "form at least of the Constitution of the Southern Confederacy was, with a few minor departures, a studied reproduction of the" national Constitution.[9]

The adoption of the Constitution was followed by a wave of prosperity, and this aided in the affection shown by the people to-

ward their governing document. Josiah Quincy, American statesman and revolutionary leader, was quick to voice the fear that "we
have grown giddy with good fortune, attributing the greatness of
our prosperity to our own wisdom, rather than to a course of
events, and a guidance over which we had no influence."[10] Although a Christian nation, America early in its history was attributing success to a document rather than God's providential work. As
history has repeatedly shown, even the slightest movement away
from the transcendancy of God manifests itself in an attachment to
the immanent, such as men or documents. As a result, an illusion is
perpetrated that it is men who determine the ultimate destiny of
nations instead of God.

Early in its history the Constitution assumed a religious
character and was afforded extreme importance. For example,
throughout the history of the United States the Bill of Rights has
consistently been regarded as important as, if not more important
than, the Decalogue itself. Even the three branches formulated in
the Constitution parallel the Christian Trinity—the President of
the executive branch is a father figure (God the Father); the Supreme Court of the judicial branch acts as the mediator (God the
Son); and the legislative branch, in its representative capacity, is
vicariously present with each citizen affording him power to act
(God the Holy Spirit). Man in every sense is religious, and he at-
taches this attribute to all that he does.

This sacred attachment to the Constitution yet prevails in
modern Christian writing.[11] Thomas Jefferson, however, warned
against affording "sanctimonious reverence" to any Constitution,
thereby deeming it "like the ark of the covenant, too sacred to be
touched."[12] Although stating that he was not for frequent changes
in the Constitution, Jefferson did feel that worship of the document
could lead to stagnation of the country's progress. From the Christian standpoint, excessive adoration of anyone or anything other
than the true God is wrong and can lead to heresy.

The Republic

The Articles of Confederation, America's first governing
document, were written and influenced by Jefferson and his classi-
cal liberal following.[13] They believed that democracy could exist

only under a weak central government. After less than a decade under the Articles, the whole structure of the federal government was approaching bankruptcy because it was impotent and detached from the state governmental systems.[14]

The liberal overtones that had pervaded the Articles were absent in the new Constitution. Although most of the revolutionary leaders supported the Constitution in the ratification debates, only eight of the fifty-six signers of the Declaration of Independence were present at the Constitutional Convention.[15]

The framers of the Constitution, after scrapping the old Articles, were staunchly opposed to democracy as the American form of government. Almost unanimous support was given to constructing a republican form of government at the Constitutional Convention.[16] The Founding Fathers knew all too well that "no society can exist without law."[17] The philosophy behind the theory of a republic is one of balanced government constructed by law. A republic holds that its officials serve in a *representative* capacity with the *consent* of the governed, as opposed to the purely democratic ideal of the *rule* of the governed. Since the framers were alarmed by the tendencies of the agrarian interests to interfere with prosperity, they were primarily concerned with balancing the government in the direction of protection for property and business.[18] Therefore, nearly all the delegates at the Constitutional Convention were constitutionalists, which meant that they were opposed to arbitrary and unrestrained government in whatever form it took.

The republican form of government is a state headed by a president or governor who is elected by a *qualified* electorate. The officials in a republic are bound to exercise their power in regard to clearly formulated laws. The basic foundation of a republic, therefore, is law. Consequently, in Article 6 the Constitution refers to itself as the "supreme law of the land."

Another important characteristic of the republic is its emphasis on the value of private property. There was an intense concern over the real-property (land) issue at the Constitutional Convention. James Madison voiced the fear that if citizens without property were given the vote it would eventually lead to an abolition of private property by the nonproperty owners.[19] The framers agreed in principle that voting should be restricted to property holders. Some of the state governments, however, were in the process of relaxing property qualifications for the vote, and the framers recognized that approval of the Constitution would be jeopardized if the federal right to vote was more restrictive than that of some of the states.[20] As a result, each individual state was left to determine the qualifications for electing members to the House of Representatives. This is the only branch of the national government in which the electorate was given a direct voice.[21]

The Aristocrats

The men who drafted the Constitution were aristocrats who believed a government should be run by highly educated and competent men. That is why a republic instead of a purely democratic system was established. A republic is primarily aristocratic in that it stresses the ideal that the better part of the people (the property owners and the educated) should govern. A pure democracy, however, throws open the gates to all, thereby in essence establishing the least qualified as the governing body.

The framers, as elitists, believed that the only way a government could survive the rigors of a fallen world was to ensure that qualified men kept hold of the reins of the state. As a result, four of the first six chief executives were Virginian aristocrats.

Any contemporary American who studies the Founding Fathers must be awed at the quality of leadership this small group of colonies produced in the late eighteenth century.[22] Such a reflection must also cause one to stop and think, "For in moral, political, and human terms we have come down a long way."[23] Eighteenth-century America was ruled by a small, highly literate elite.

The aristocrats instituted the electoral college to protect the elitist control of the government. The framers abhorred the idea of political parties with their warring factions controlled by the popular will. George Washington in his farewell address expressed the thought that strong party spirits could lead to the emergence of a dictator.

It was never the intention of men like Thomas Jefferson, John Adams, and Alexander Hamilton to suggest that the common or average man should assert himself as a person equal in judgment, in discernment, or in knowledge to those competent to serve him in government.[24] They believed in a system founded on free enterprise and stringent competition, which system would produce quality people competent enough to administer the government of the freest nation on the earth.

The Legal Class

The men who molded the American government believed that essential to the longevity of America was a foundation in law. Without law, they believed there could be no liberty or freedom. In addition, the foundation of American law at that time was Christian theology, which was based on the Scriptures.

The legalistic temperament of America was well set before the Revolution. Puritanism with its moralistic influence had previously conquered the minds of the nation. This moralistic and legalistic viewpoint was largely responsible for the careful wording of the Constitution.

Nearly half the signers of the Declaration of Independence were lawyers. As the aristocratic class that had born the framers passed from the American scene, lawyers filled the vacancy left and, therefore, became a class with immense power. Historically, the result of this is that over two-thirds of those men holding the office of president have been lawyers or have been connected with the legal profession. Also, between one-half and two-thirds of the seats in Congress have usually been filled with lawyers.[25]

The French historian Alexis de Tocqueville, a Christian, was astounded at the power the legal profession exercised in America. He said lawyers resembled "the Egyptian priests, being, as they were, the only interpreter of an occult science."[26]

The Heresy

As a child grows up in the United States, he hears over and over again that this country is a democracy. This was not true when this nation was founded under the Constitution. Unfortunately, being fallen men, we repeat creeds from habit without ever really analyzing their content. This is easily understood because heresies are "almost always very near to truth."[27] Unfortunately, heresies usually lead to illusion.

The Founding Fathers were ardent subscribers to John Locke's theory that a government's primary duty is the preservation of property. This view was followed by John Jay, Alexander

Hamilton, and James Madison (to name a few), who believed in the fundamental inequality of men.[28] In view of the obvious failure of Jeffersonian democracy via the Articles of Confederation, they had no real inhibitions about making their views public. Therefore, during the debates concerning the ratification of the Constitution these men wrote *The Federalist Papers,* which opted for a stronger government founded on laws—a republic, not a democracy.

In recent decades the leftist element has avidly proclaimed that the Constitution is purely a democratic document. The renowned constitutional-law authority Edward S. Corwin, to the contrary, said, "The attribution of supremacy of the Constitution on the ground of its rootage in popular will represents a comparatively late outgrowth of American constitutional theory."[29] Corwin said that supremacy was accorded the Constitution because of its content and the "embodiment of essential and unchanging justice."[30] This emphasis on law stands directly opposed to pure democracy's theory of changing and evolving laws as the people dictate.

Early Opposition

The Pilgrim fathers were certainly neither democrats nor liberals. They were Puritans, which means they were Calvinists. There is no democratic egalitarianism ("all is equal") in Calvinist theology. The Calvinist doctrine of predestination separates mankind into those who are damned and those who are saved. The elect of God partake of divine favor while the nonelect are cursed.

In addition, the basic idea upon which the Puritan political system was founded was that church members alone could have political rights—that is, the privileges of voting. This ensured that the Puritan commonwealth could be nothing but an oligarchy (rule by a few). Pure democracy, on the other hand, requires political equality (voting privileges) regardless of property ownership or other restrictions. As Karl Marx pointed out, private property, being basic to any free government, is lost when the nonproperty owner legislates over the property owner. This happens when the nonproperty owners gain majority control. Calvinistic theology is directly opposed to pure democracy.

Even after the War of Independence the thirteen colonies remained nondemocratic. Only property owners could vote, and it wasn't until 1791 that these restrictions began to recede.

It must be remembered that the term *democratic* appears neither in the Declaration of Independence nor in the Constitution. Actually, when the Constitution is analyzed in its original form, the document is found to be a serious attempt to establish a government mixed with democratic, aristocratic, and monarchical elements—a government of checks and balances. Basically, the Constitution erects a republic but ever since its inception the American Republic has been exposed to democratizing influences.

The Founding Fathers, as the educated elite of their era, rejected democracy outright. Their contempt was intensified when totalitarian repression became the dominating feature of the French Revolution. Many of the framers, including George Washington and James Madison, would have subscribed to John Adams' sharp remark that democracy was "the most ignoble, unjust, and detestable form of government."[31] Years later, in 1815, Adams, the second president of the United States, warned his countrymen, "Democracy has never been and never can be so desirable as aristocracy or monarchy, but while it lasts, is more bloody than either. Remember, democracy never lasts long. It soon wastes, exhausts and murders itself. There never was a democracy that did not commit suicide."[32]

Rule of the People

The American Republic was to be a government administered with the *consent* of the governed. This ideal is clearly opposed to *rule* of the governed. The administrations of George Washington and John Adams proceeded on the basis that the government was organized and clothed with power to rule according to the Constitution. The democratic theorists, however, insist that the people, basically meaning themselves, have an inherent right to rule.

Democracy is a Greek word composed of *demos* (the people) and *kratos* (power—in a strong, almost brutal sense). The milder form of the latter Greek term would be *arche,* which implies leadership rather than rule. Hence, "monarchy" is a fatherlike rule in the interest of the common good of the people, whereas "monocracy" is a one-man tyranny.

A basic foundation of a democracy is what has been called majority rule. The repression of forty-nine percent of the people by fifty-one percent or of one percent by ninety-nine percent is most regrettable, but it certainly is not "undemocratic." Obviously, the whole people is never the ruler; instead, a majority usually rules through its representatives. We see then that the phrase "rule of the people" is misleading. The majority rules over the minority, a situation reminiscent of the famous phrase from George Orwell's *Animal Farm*, "All animals are equal, but some are more equal than others."

Pure democratic ideology relies heavily on the slogan *vox populi, vox dei,* which literally means "the voice of the people is the voice of God." God views this type of thinking as a rejection of Him (I Samuel 8:7). As depicted in the eighth chapter of the first book of Samuel, the consequence of rejecting God is becoming subject to other fallen men. Therefore, man's children and property are taken from him by his new ruler. Eventually, man seeks God, but Samuel clearly says that "the Lord will not answer . . . in that day" (I Samuel 8:18). Once God and His biblical standards are rejected for a pure democracy, then the nation comes under judgment—"The Lord nullifies the counsel of the nations; He frustrates the plans of the peoples" (Psalm 33:10).

The Crucifixion and Democracy

Socrates committed suicide shortly before he was to be executed by the state. There were several charges brought by the government against him, one of which was that he constantly quoted Homer and Hesiod against morality and democracy.[33] Not only the democratic government but the people also were opposed to Socrates, and without exaggeration he can be called a victim of democracy—*vox populi* (the voice of the people).

It has been said that Western civilization rests on two deaths—the death of Socrates and the death of Christ.[34] Indeed, the crucifixion was a democratic event. When our Lord was brought before Pilate and said He was a witness to the truth, the governor, as a true agnostic, asked Him, "What is truth?" And without waiting for an answer, he passed Him by and consulted "the people." The *vox populi* condemned our Lord to death, as it had Socrates some three centuries earlier.

God the Father and Democracy

The pure democratic ideology is automatically hostile to all hierarchies and differentiations. All things must be leveled and reduced to a station of "equality."

The democratic stand is for brotherhood as against what is deemed a heresy—fatherhood. Under pure democratic governments the father image is assailed. Theologically, this invites a revision of the concept of God as Father, ending in a rejection of the Trinity. Early in the history of Christianity antitrinitarian faiths sprang up which advocated the three ideals that eventually became the shibboleth of the bloodbath called the French Revolution—liberty, equality, and fraternity (brotherhood).

Applying this concept to the political sphere meant questioning monarchy as well as any other form of government with a monarchic head. Fortunately, this was not the philosophical or religious ideal of the Founding Fathers as they erected a monarchal head to lead their government—a president, or chief of state, as he is called.

French Catholic philosopher Jean Lacroix sees in democracy first the revolt against God, resulting in the revolt against all fatherhood. Said Lacroix, "One could say that to a large extent the present democratic movement is the murder of the father."[35]

Jerome Frank, influential judge and author, seemingly would not disagree with Lacroix's position. He said that "modern" civilization demands a mind free of father governance.

Mom, or even "Big Brother," can be more easily understood by the modern American mind than can father. For instance, Uncle Sam is not a father but essentially a New England bachelor.

Democracy, therefore, requires "total brotherhood," which eventually eliminates fatherhood. As this country moves deep into the democratic ideal, the disappearance of the father as well as the father image will be readily apparent.

The Family and Democracy

The disappearance of the father image is seen also in the family. In fact, the family is a fundamental enemy of democracy because of its resistance to leveling. For example, within the biblical family there is a basic inequality of roles. The father is instituted as the head of the family. All other roles are subordinate to the father's federal headship. The child is taught his first government in the family, and it is here that the child also learns to govern himself. In fact, self-government is an extension of the family. Destroy the family and self-government is destroyed.

The family is also the foundation of private property within a culture. Private property evidences and promotes a basic inequality among men because some have large property holdings while others have none. Likewise, inheritance is scorned in a democracy because it perpetuates private property by passing wealth from generation to generation. Inheritance taxes are so steep for this is a way of collecting rent on property passed to the next generation.

This age has seen the greatest attack in the history of the United States on the family. As an institution, the family is passing away. Only within Christendom has it thrived, but even there it is suffering from democratization. The public school has largely emerged as a substitute for the disappearing family in the modern society. State control of education, as history instructs us, declares the death of the biblical family. The death of the family, however, is a product of the death of man. The death of the family is sure to lead to the death of the culture.

The Inner Light

The father of modern democracy is Jean Jacques Rousseau. He was a French philosopher whose ideas heavily influenced the chaos that resulted in the French Revolution of 1789.

The first characteristic of a democracy is that it is an exclusive religion.[36] Rousseau became its first prophet, espousing the religious doctrine of the "inner light."

In his famous treatise entitled *Social Contract,* Rousseau states that there is a contract between the people and the ruler, but it is not an agreement by the people to obey the ruler. Instead, it is an agreement by the individual citizens to subordinate their judgment, rights, and powers to the needs and judgment of the community as a whole. The sovereign power, therefore, lies not in God or a ruler, but in the *general will* of the community (or the majority).

The sovereignty of the people may be delegated in part and for a time, but it can never be totally surrendered.[37]

The people, collectively, become god because the "inner light" within them gives them an instinctive knowledge of the natural law. The state, or government, which is the people collectively, exercises this instinctive knowledge.

The theory behind pure democracy is that if the people agree to do something it becomes permissible—whether it be homosexuality or consuming drugs—because they possess the "inner light." If a law or moral restriction does not suit their tastes, then the people, as the sovereign, can change it. Restrictions of any kind eventually become chains to the people. The way to throw off chains in the past has been to call for revolution.

Rousseau dangerously asserted that there must be what he called compulsory "sentiments of sociability" promulgated and enforced by the state. In other words, all men must be in unity, and there can be no inequality among men. The religious idea espoused here is that the sovereign people must be totally unified just as the Christian God is. Imitation of God, however, always carries a satanic flavor.

According to Rousseau, the greatest crime in a democratic state is antisocial behavior. Differentiation, delineation, or differences of any kind that cause inequality among men must be rejected, and in their place the "unity of equality" is inserted. Rousseau said, "Anything that breaks social unity is worthless; all institutions which set a man in conflict with himself are worthless." To Rousseau Christianity was contrary to the social spirit because it was "so far from attaching the hearts of all citizens to the state." Instead, he remarked, "It detaches them from it, as from all earthly things."

To Karl Marx and Rousseau alike, the belief fundamental to Christianity that there is a citizenship of godly people transcending the citizenship of the earth was deemed the most asocial of all possible sentiments.[38] That God elected certain individuals to be His own chosen people contradicts Rousseau's unity of equality. Also, the scriptural principle that teaches the existence of heaven and hell is opposed to pure democracy because this doctrine instead of uniting men separates them.

The Christian church eventually catches the ire of the democratic state. The church is the pillar and the ground of the truth for the Christian people who are specially separated from the non-Christian world. This scriptural concept flows against the grain of the process of democratization. The logic of the democratic government is that it cannot tolerate any church that "is more, or other, than a domestic chaplain of the state."[39] Therefore, a government that operates on democratic principles will seek to reduce the church to nothing but a formal institution with no real significance.

The true God is a criminal and an outcast in a state ruled by people who lift themselves to the position of a god. As a result, God becomes a wanted being whose every presence is sought out to be destroyed. This, as we know, is an outgrowth of "the separation illusion." *this is happening to God's people*

As man struggles for freedom apart from God, he finds himself enslaved by the very government that grants him his "freedom." As the state grants rights it has to enlarge to enforce the rights it grants. Before man realizes that he has been worshipping a monster, he finds himself in its chains.

The late Will Herberg, a leading critic and a Drew University professor, said most Americans are unaware of any tension between this "religion of democracy" and their own faith.[40] But, he added, it is "idolatry" for these Americans—however innocent their intent—"to see American civil religion as somehow standing above and beyond the biblical religions of Judaism and Christianity and somehow finding a place for them in its overarching unity."[41]

Lord Percy of Newcastle was right in concluding that democracy "is a fake worship whose sincerest devotees, approaching their idol shrine with the most unselfish aspirations, wake from their trance of adoration to find themselves bound unawares to the service of devils."[42]

Equality Before God?

A well-known cliché asserts that, although men are neither identical nor equal physically or intellectually, men are at least "equal in the eyes of God." Nothing could be further from the truth. The true Christian faith teaches that all men are not equally loved by God. For example, the Scriptures tell us that Christ loved Peter more than Judas. It is also obvious that Hitler and Luther were not equals in the eyes of God. If they had been, Christianity would no longer make any sense because the sinner would be equal with the saint and to be evil would be the same as to be good.

The "all men are equal in the eyes of God" philosophy is an example of how democratic thought has polluted the doctrines of many theologians. Freedom is spoken of several times in the holy Scriptures, but equality is never mentioned.

While man's physical and intellectual inferiorities and superiorities can be determined with some accuracy, his spiritual status is much more difficult to ascertain. We simply do not know who is nearer to God because we have no way of seeing inside the man. It lies with God to choose whom He desires to be His. It is definitely not left to man to reduce all men to the same level before the God who has clearly differentiated amongst His creation. For man to determine otherwise is blasphemy.

Equality and Opportunity

In a concrete sense not even a totalitarian tyranny could bring about what is called "equality of opportunity."[43] For example, no country could decree that a child at birth should have "equal parents." They may be equal as to the wealth of all other parents in the country, but could they provide equal heredity or the same nutrition as other parents?

The cry for an identical and equal education has been raised again and again in democracies, and the existence of Christian education has been deemed undemocratic. In an attempt to provide "equality of opportunity" egalitarians have advocated not only intensive schooling but also boarding school for all. This means that children are to be taken from the private home and collectively educated twenty-four hours a day. Collective education is the system presently employed by the Soviet Union, where it is predicted that more than ninety percent of all children past the age of six will be in boarding schools after 1980.[44] Even this measure will fall short of equality of opportunity, unless one disregards the capacity and skills of the individual. When this happens, a general decline of all levels then sets in.

Equality at all costs becomes the driving principle behind pure democratic government. Its two chief agents are the tax gatherer and the technologist. The one seeks to reduce men to manageable units of assessment for the collection of revenue, the other to manageable units for handling the instruments of production.[45] From there it is easy, as the state grows, to extend the leveling process to all children, for example, making them manageable units for the purposes of a comprehensive system of state-controlled schooling.[46]

The Mark of the Beast

Egalitarianism ("all is equal") cannot make much headway without the use of force. During the French Revolution in 1789, a team of citizens went about knocking down all the steeples that were higher than the other buildings. Inequality in any form had to be democratized (the ultimate equality is found in the graveyard).

Perfect equality, naturally, is only possible in a governmental system of total slavery. Since nature, which is free from artificial restraints, has no bias against even the most apparent inequalities, force must be utilized to establish equality. The use of force in most cases, however, limits and eventually destroys freedom.

There are real antagonism and conflict between freedom and forced equality. Nevertheless, democracy demands that all men equate in unity. This drive to equality is a result of what Erik von Kuehnelt-Leddihn calls "freedom from fear."[47] The common man, out of fear of another man's superiority, seeks to bring the superior man down to his inferior level. A democracy eventually brings about an inferior race of men through what it calls "forced equality."

The unassimilable, or he who fails to "fit in," must therefore be eliminated. Eccentricities and superiorities are asocial as well as any form of life that is differentiated from the masses. In the end all life becomes a privilege, and all antisocial life must be rooted out. "This is, indeed, democracy's characteristic Mark of the Beast."[48]

The purging of the antisocial one is the "mark of the beast." *Antisocial* is defined as anyone or anything that asserts individuality as opposed to unity and equality. Christianity offends "the beast." In the past blood has run like rivers because Christianity would not be reduced to the eye-level of every other religion.

The ultimate conclusion of a government that seeks to effec-tuate democracy is totalitarian government. Rousseau's principles were carried to their zenith during the French Revolution, when the true God was declared dead and reason was enthroned as god. The Reign of Terror memorializes those principles. The ideals of the French Revolution were absorbed by Marx, whose philosophy became the bedrock foundation of the Soviet Union.

Rousseau's state (or government) was to be but temporary, until everything was leveled and the antisocial aspects purged. While it is purging the antisocial, the state calmly proclaims, "Peace, peace!" But as Jeremiah answered the false prophets who met him with such a cry, "There is no peace" (Jeremiah 6:14).

Under a pure democracy the purging government is always present and lurking in the shadows to eradicate that form of life which claims to be different from all other forms. The idea of indi-viduality, therefore, is the worst enemy of democracy.

The ultimate conclusion of pure democracy is the USSR. Ac-cording to Jacques Ellul, there are more differences between the United States of 1910 and the United States today than there are between this country at the present time and the Soviet Union.[49] The fact that the United States is being democratized has caused some to remark that post-America is looking more like the Soviet Union day by day.

It is time that we open our eyes to see where we are going so that we can have time to reconstruct the system. As a Paul McCartney verse concluded, "I'm back in the USSR. You don't know how lucky you are, boys."[50]

The People Versus Genesis

As part of the curse that had come upon man following the Fall, God established the first government (Genesis 3:16). As sin entered the world, chaos became a reality. To prevent total anarchy God introduced the institution of the state to keep order because man was now a depraved sinner. Man cannot govern himself and so must resist his impulse of doing away with all authority over him. To do so would be to repudiate the curse that God placed upon mankind, and this in turn would be a repudiation of God.

If its doctrines are strictly followed, democracy requires that the people govern and eventually dissolve the state. This philosophy is an apparent attack against God because it is an attempt to throw off the bondage of the curse with revolution and disobedience instead of with regeneration. This is autonomous man erecting "the separation illusion" in order to go his own way without God. As we have seen, this unreality leads man to utter destruction.

The basic form of government as established by God immediately following the Fall was a monarchy (rule of one man in the interest of the common good). The Western mentality has an unnatural fear of monarchies, but monarchies can be just as effective and benevolent as any other form of government. The effect of a monarchy, like any other type of government, depends upon the man or men who rule it. The crucial issue is whether they are a regenerate or unregenerate people. If regenerate, the governmental system will be administered according to biblical standards. If not, the people will separate themselves from biblical revelation in an attempt to determine their own fate.

As recognized by Aristotle and Plato, a curious evolution (or "evilution") of governmental forms occurs depending on man's willingness to submit to rule. The Scriptures require the Christian to submit to the government he finds himself under (Romans 13:1-7). As man has rebelled, the governmental form has evolved from a monarchy to an aristocracy (rule of a group in the interest of the common good). The aristocracy evolves into a republic (rule of the better part of the people in the interest of the common good), which in turn evolves into a democracy (rule of the least qualified for their own benefit). A democracy eventually evolves into a totalitarian regime (rule of one man to his own advantage), and the totalitarian regime returns again into a monarchy. This last stage seems to be impossible in the modern world since Big Brother is incapable of being a father.

This is not an absolute or fixed movement from one form of government to another. Man lives not in a closed system, but operates within an open system. Within the open system God works and moves according to His design, and He determines what form of rule man will be under at any particular time. Also, according to his relationship to God, man can determine what form of government he has to submit to. Basically, an ungodly people will find themselves under a tyranny. As the godly retain control, the tyranny recedes and freedom returns.

God will bless a monarchy, aristocracy, or republic depending on the peoples' relationship to Him. A truly godly people cannot establish a democracy since it is an unscriptural form of government. The United States today is caught in limbo between a republic and a democracy. A mixed form such as this can operate effectively depending, again, upon the relationship of the people with God. The United States, however, has become a secularized nation, and as the country moves further into secularization it moves closer to tyranny.

"Believe, Fight, Obey"

A basic difference between a pure democracy and a republic is that the latter has a basic foundation in law, law such as our Constitution, for instance. A democracy requires constant change according to the general will of the majority.

A republic was intended by the Founding Fathers. Democratic thought, especially in the form of Marxism, has permeated the philosophy of government in the United States. And democracy leads to a totalitarian state or government. The state is necessary to purge the antisocial, and most communistic countries run true to this pattern.

Another problem presently faces the United States. A strong foundation in law has from the beginning kept this country from slipping into pure democracy. The foundation now finds itself susceptible to erosion by fascism.

Fascism is an authoritarian state in which the government controls every facet of life while crushing opposition by means of secret police. Although proclaiming its hatred for communism, fascism shares communism's abhorrence of constitutional procedure, its disregard of the individual human being and its insistence that the state is supreme.[51] Fascism persecutes its enemies, both real and imagined, with the same ruthlessness that occurred in Stalin's Russia. Censorship, political police, concentration camps, the rule of the billyclub are all practices of fascism.[52]

Fascism is extremely deceptive in infiltrating a particular government; it retains the form, or shell, of the previous governmental system while according it little validity. The danger is that fascism can assume control before most realize it has even been present.

That danger faces the United States today. The basic forms of the Republic are still with us, but they are becoming mere forms without content. For example, a man retains the title to his property, but the government taxes him nearly as much as the property is worth. If a man is taxed up to eighty percent of his property's value, the government is then deriving the income from the property, not the individual. In actuality, the titleholder is paying rent to the government for the privilege of holding the paper title. Although the individual is left with the title to the property, the government acts as if it owned the property.

With each election the political parties become more form than content. The candidates avoid issues so that neither will have to face them. In the end no choice is left, only an alternative between the lesser of two evils. When the newly elected politician takes office, the same programs and technicians are there that existed under his predecessor. Little in the way of change may be expected through the electoral process. If, for example, a newly elected president wanted to eradicate the welfare system he would very likely face a revolution.

This secularization of government is a consequence of the denial of God. Such a government unfailingly tends to regard the people as automatons. Gradually, the fallen men who run the government see other men as things to manipulate. Martin Luther warned of this: "Where there are no people who have been made wise through the Word and the laws, there bears, lions, goats, and dogs hold public office and head the economy."[53]

When fascist Benito Mussolini was ruling in Rome, public buildings everywhere carried the admonition to loyal Italians: "Believe, fight, obey."[54] Presumably this was intended to inspire support for "Il Duce" and his regime. What it really meant was: *believe* (what Mussolini tells you); *fight* (for Mussolini and his backers); *obey* (Mussolini).[55] Put this way, the motto becomes a formula for subverting all religion and human decency.

Fascism, so dangerous because so difficult in its initial phases to detect, has progressed far enough in the United States to be detectable. Either it needs to be halted or the country may be in for a terrific upheaval.

The General Will and the Supreme Court

In the famous 1803 case of *Marbury* v. *Madison* Chief Justice John Marshall established the Supreme Court as the ultimate lawmaker in the United States. This case held that the Court has the power to review acts of Congress and declare them void if they are repugnant to the Constitution.[56] As a result, the Court becomes the sole interpreter of what the Constitution does and does not allow.

The basic foundation of the American Republic is law—the Constitution. If the Court is the sole interpreter of the basic document of law, then the Court determines what is law. The Court, therefore, not only executes a judicial function, but also performs a legislative function. Any legislative acts, however, are to be administered in a representative capacity under the Constitution. This is impossible with the Supreme Court because the justices are not elected but are appointed by the President.

Law has its origin in religion.[57] The Supreme Court, therefore, makes a religious determination when it decides a case. Being humanists, the justices decide what is right or wrong on the basis of what their religion holds. The religion of humanity, however, is a relativistic religion; it merely depends on each circumstance whether a particular act is right or wrong. This philosophy is a continuation of Oliver Wendell Holmes' theory that law is experience, not logic.

Not surprisingly, since the late forties the Supreme Court has been deciding cases in the pure democratic and humanist terms of Rousseau's general will. But with this difference. The Court is deciding cases not by the general will of the majority, but by the general will of the minority (or interest groups).

Governments administered by pure democratic, humanistic principles are highly susceptible to interest-group control. Men are lumped collectively as the masses. Whoever controls the state, even if his decisions violate the so-called general will, rules. The Court takes pains to read the minority mind in reaching its decisions. Polls conducted immediately following the 1962 prayer decision indicated that a clear majority disagreed with the Court, but the majority was overruled.

There is nothing wrong with protection of minority interests. However, when the Constitution is utilized by interpretation to accomplish the wishes of the presiding justices it then renders the Constitution worthless. No longer is it law; it is relativism. There is no morality because morality deals with *absolute* right and wrong. If there is no morality then an institution like the Supreme Court can adulterate the basic document of its country without thinking twice.

Again, Martin Luther was on target: "I know for certain that we theologians and jurists must stay, or all the rest will go down with us. When the theologians disappear, God's Word disappears, and only heathen, aye, nothing but devils, remain. When the jurist disappears, and peace goes away with it, and nothing but robbery, murder, crime, and violence, aye, nothing but wild beasts remain."[58]

A Natural Aristocracy

Although Thomas Jefferson espoused democratic rhetoric from time to time, he was an aristocrat who knew that the basic premise to freedom was achievement and excellence. Jefferson recognized that little is left of liberty if freedom to excel is denied. Therefore, he was basically opposed to democracy with its attendant reduction of all things to their lowest common denominator.

Jefferson once remarked, "There is a natural aristocracy among men. The grounds of this are virtue and talents."[59] Jefferson contrasted his natural aristocracy with "an artificial aristocracy, founded on wealth and birth, without either virtue or talents."[60] Natural aristocracy was for Jefferson "the most precious gift of nature."[61]

A government freed from destructive egalitarianism ("all is equal"), says John Silber, president of Boston University, "provides a society in which the wisest, the best, and the most dedicated assume positions of leadership, offering foresight, direction and energy on which its future depends."[62] In other words, competition that recognizes a basic inequality among men is vital to a progressive and free government.

Silber also notes it is a mistake to claim that every institution within the state should be democratic. "That the government must be democratic follows from the principle that it derives its authority from the consent of the governed. But it does not follow that every institution within a democracy should be organized democratically. In fact, most institutions ought to be run on an elitist basis—that is, decisions within them ought to be made by those most qualified to make them . . . as long as intelligence is better than stupidity and knowledge than ignorance, no university can run except on an elitist basis."[63]

John Silber is committed to democracy but feels the bite of democratization, and rather than recognize that our system is a republic he contradicts himself by stating that "not . . . every institution within a democracy should be . . . democratic." The indoctrination of the ideals of the democratic philosophy even plagues the most intelligent citizens, and the only way to escape illusion is to recognize that the United States was founded as a republic.

To develop a natural aristocracy, the Founding Fathers greatly emphasized education. Madison, Jefferson, and Adams all insisted that the value of education could not be exaggerated because it is the condition on which effective self-government depends.[64] Moreover, the education they had in mind was a liberal education "rich not merely in the study of sciences but also in the study of morals."[65] The study of religion was essential because historically morals have been a religious concern. These men would have abhorred the secularized educational system in the United States today.

Post-America

Karl Marx said, "The criticism of religion is the premise of all criticism." He saw Christianity as a stumblingblock to communism. Accordingly, Marxism vehemently attacks and criticizes Christianity and its antileveling doctrines.

Through such criticism, Marx believed religion would end "with the doctrine that man is the supreme being for man." This leads to a denial of the existence of God, and eventually leads to the denial of man as man.

Intimacy, familiarity, and lack of reverence have become the dominant themes of American life with the passing of Christianity. Nothing else smooths the way to totalitarianism (rule by a state that controls everything) more than these traits. "The democratic idea that any man is as good as his neighbor automatically destroys the vital tension, the desire to emulate and 'reach up to.' Even when practiced with as much engaging friendliness as in America, its main result is to nip in the bud any form of self-improvement."[66]

While President, Dwight D. Eisenhower remarked, "Our government makes no sense unless it is founded in a deeply religious faith—and I don't care what it is."[67] He was right about the need for faith, but inestimably wrong about his indifference to religious preference. History proves that wherever freedom has flourished Christianity has been the basic faith. And wherever the true God is denied, there is doom. Proverbs 11:14 accents this point: "Where there is no guidance, the people fall."

The iron-willed Puritans were accustomed to raising their eyes to God while reverencing Him, becoming all the while more spiritualized. The modern descendants of the Puritans have lowered their sights to the horizontal, to the eye level of the common man. This steady process of secularization, humanization, and vulgarization has destroyed a great deal of the "vital and creative tension" that has been characteristic of the United States in the past. More frightening, however, is the historical fact that a long trend of secularism leads to totalitarianism.

The Christian religion was the faith of early America, and it was ever present throughout the first century of American history. In 1835, the French historian Alexis de Tocqueville, while visiting the United States, reported, "Upon my arrival in the United States, the religious aspect of the country was the first thing that struck my attention." And in 1848 he eloquently remarked:

> *America is still the place where the Christian religion has kept the greatest real power over men's souls; and nothing better demonstrates how useful and natural it is to man, since the country where it now has the widest sway is both the most enlightened and the freest.... They [the clergy] are at pains to keep out of the affairs and not mix in the ... parties. One cannot therefore say that in the United States religion influences the laws or political opinions in detail, but it does direct mores, and by regulating domestic life it helps to regulate the state.*[68]

In his famous treatise, *Democracy in America*, Tocqueville equates freedom with Christianity. He also equates Christianity with America. In other words, if Christianity is separated from America then America no longer exists, and instead, something foreign comes to the forefront—Post-America.

Historians like the late Perry Miller tell us that the Great Awakening, a spiritual revival of the 1740s, paved the way for the American Revolution.* Under such eloquent spiritual teaching sat many of those young people who would soon be called the Founding Fathers of America.[69] From that era came John Adams, who wrote, "Statesmen may plan and speculate liberty, but it is religion and morality alone upon which freedom can securely stand. A patriot must be a religious man."[70]

James Russell Lowell, an American poet and statesman of the late nineteenth century, was asked, "How long do you think the American Republic will indure?" Lowell replied, "So long as the ideas of its Founding Fathers continue to be dominant."[71]

One must be honest in saying that Tocqueville's America is not modern America. We live in a post-American culture, something vastly different from that which the Founding Fathers intended or even imagined.

The people of the United States have grasped the European mind, and like the magnet that cannot escape the metal fragments that cling to it, neither can this country escape the curse of European thought without returning to the true God.

With rare keenness Tocqueville pointedly commented, "Unbelievers in Europe attack Christians more as political than as religious enemies; they hate the faith as the opinion of a party much more than as a mistaken belief, and they reject the clergy less because they are the representatives of God than because they are the friends of authority."[72] Christianity is a political threat to the state or government that believes itself to be god. The Christian religion asserts that there is only one true God whom all men are to serve.

Post-America has fallen prey to the separation illusion—the idea that it can deny God and yet survive. This is insane; nay worse, suicidal. For as God has said, "All those who hate me love death" (Proverbs 8:36).

---

*The Great Awakening, with its accent on the *individual's* need for salvation, engendered a change in many Christians' outlook on the organized church. A greater freedom of conscience was a fruit of this changed perspective. These factors, coupled with the Calvinistic and Separatist influence already existing in the colonial mind, proved potent forces for resistance.

≀ 3 ≀

The Shift

*After the Civil War phase the United States are
really only now entering the revolutionary phase, and the
European wiseacres, who believe in the omnipotence
of [President] Johnson, will soon be disillusioned.*

Karl Marx

*The so-called Civil War was in reality a second American
Revolution.*

Charles A. Beard

The Constitution was devoid of a Bill of Rights when it
emerged from the Philadelphia Convention in 1787. This omission
was the basis of the most crucial and serious criticisms of the new
Constitution by the state conventions (although they finally ratified
it). It was felt that a Bill of Rights "would protect fundamental
rights against interference by the new federal government."[1] This
fear of Big Brother eventually produced the Bill of Rights as the
first ten amendments to the Constitution in 1791.

These amendments were appended to the original Constitution
as restrictions on the federal government. For example, the First
Amendment states that the federal government cannot prohibit the
freedom of speech or the freedom of religion. The framers believed
the government that governs least was the best government.

The Constitution was written by men who knew that the only
way effectively to restrain the federal government was through the
existence of strong state governments. They realized that the centralization of power in the federal government would end in a des-

potic administration. The accumulation of vast power in Washington, D.C. was to James Madison "the very definition of tyranny." Madison said, "The powers delegated by the proposed Constitution to the federal government are few and defined. Those which are to remain in the state governments are numerous and indefinite." In fact, the Constitution makes eighty grants of power to the federal government while levying 115 prohibitions against it. To Congress it yields twenty grants of power while imposing seventy restraints.

The tentacles of control now extend from the District of Columbia to the smallest town in the United States. How has this come about? As illustrated in the preceding chapter, America was a nation of laws. Therefore, the way to change the country was to change the foundation and meaning of law. This is why the Supreme Court has been so effective in molding generation after generation.

The Supreme Court, especially during the Warren era (1953–1969), has been guilty beyond a reasonable doubt of willfully substituting fantasy for fact and for failing to investigate history. The greatest untruth promulgated by the Court was its role in the misinterpretation of the Fourteenth Amendment to the Constitution. Exercising a god-function, the Court radically altered the course of this country's government which, in turn, restricted our liberty that is so dear.

The Bill of Rights was designed by the Founding Fathers as an assurance of freedom. However, it is now being utilized to restrict and render the states impotent. Instead of a Bill of Rights it has become a "Bill of Chains" to the state governments.

To understand the change that was wrought in the Constitution and the resultant change in the American government, the revolution that carried the metamorphosis from America to post-America must be studied. Before going any further it is necessary to look briefly at the fiasco that precipitated the post-American consciousness.

The Second American Revolution

The Founding Fathers formed a government upon law that would suit their aristocratic tastes. The Civil War, however, destroyed the last remnant of aristocratic rule and way of life in America, "and it [the Civil War] was instinctively understood in this sense by the entire English-speaking world."[2]

The South emerged from the Civil War stained and bruised, and still carries this tainted image over a century later. Much of this image is illusion. For instance, the only Jewish senators before the war were from the South. This liberalism was largely the attitude of self-confident aristocrats who didn't have to bow to the pressure of democratic public opinion. In fact, as historian Amaury de Riencourt points out, "Only one Southerner in ten owned slaves and most of the slaves were held by a small group of a few thousand wealthy planters who perpetrated the manners and traditions of the Virginian Founding Fathers, the aristocratic gentlemen whose remarkable qualities had made America's independence possible."[3]

Basically, there were three factors responsible for the Civil War: politics, economics, and theology. These three things split the country deeply enough to force the two factions to go to war to perpetuate their causes.

Politically, the North was committed to the idea of democracy with its leveling of all things to their lowest common denominator. The South, however, posed problems for the northern egalitarians, who eventually regarded the Negro slave as a class oppressed by an iron-handed southern aristocracy. This estimate was but partially true; only a very small minority of citizens in the South owned slaves. This is not to say that the existing slavery wasn't bad, but to say that history has been distorted somewhat in this area. Regardless of the confusing mixture of fact and fantasy that characterized this era, the conflicting ideals of the North and South made war inevitable.

The Agreement with Hell

The abolitionists attacked the Constitution and called it "an agreement with hell."[4] This attack was precipitated by Article I, Section 2 of the Constitution, which makes a slave three-fifths of a person and treats him as property.

The abolitionists were a group of radicals who, in seeking to free the slaves, "were apt to journey very close to anarchism."[5]

While idealizing the Negro, the abolitionists sought to usher in a utopian millennium.[6] Being revolutionaries, they sought any means to bring about the desired result—including war. But fallen men are incapable of building utopia, concludes Eugene Methvin, "even if they agree on a design."[7]

The abolitionists clearly saw that to further equality for all, the federal government would have to exercise more power and control over the individual states. This meant coercion. The South naturally rested its laurels on states' rights as opposed to a large central government, claiming this was supported by the Constitution. That position was valid to some degree. Alexander Hamilton gives credence to the states' rights argument in *Federalist,* number 28:

> *It may safely be received as an axiom in our political system, that the state governments will, in all possible contingencies, afford complete security against invasions of the public liberty by the national authority* ... *they can at once adopt a regular plan of opposition [secession] in which they can combine all the resources of the community. They can readily communicate with each other in the different states, and unite their common forces for the protection of their common liberty.*[8]

Since the founding of the Republic, the South had controlled the presidency, the Congress, and the Supreme Court. As the North grew economically independent and powerful, northern business interests sought more political influence.

The North developed into an industrial complex while the South remained mostly agrarian in nature. The North depended on machines for economic stability while the South depended on farming for income. The northern business interests pushed for the replacement of man-fuel by coal and oil fuel—human muscles by mechanized gadgets.

In the struggle for control of the national government the northern Republicans moved for more stringent federal controls to protect their economic interests. Their attempts to establish a national bank, to subsidize shipping and business enterprise, and to implement protective tariffs were met with sharp opposition by the southern democrats. The South saw all the federal programs as an attempt to destroy state sovereignty in favor of a centralized government. Therefore, they emphasized that it was unconstitutional to "nationalize" the states since the tenor of the Constitution was centered rather on local control of government than on central or national control.

Light and Darkness

The most neglected irritant of the conflict was the theological issue. As many a sociologist will affirm, any particular culture is merely the outgrowth of the current religion of that society.

Modern historians have seldom given theology its proper place in the determination of American history. "The recognition of the importance of intellectual forces in the stream of history must be followed by one other step, namely, the realization that the intellectual development of a people is not an entity in itself, but, in turn, depends upon their theology, or lack thereof."[9]

Man is never irreligious. He always has faith. The primary question is: In what does he place his faith? And secondarily: What is his source of regeneration and worship? Therefore, we must always ask: Is the religion of a particular culture the religion of the true God, or the religion of humanity?

A man's faith either divides him from or unites him with other men. Throughout history men have always been sharply separated because of a difference in religion. In this respect, the Scriptures clearly delineate two spiritual races. In terms of antithesis, one is either the son of God or the son of Satan. These are the two basic religions. Between this light and darkness exists the great chasm among men.

Spiritual Enemies

Calvinism (the faith of the Puritans) and its theological doctrines dominated the North American culture for one and a half centuries. As the church began receding in the first quarter of the nineteenth century through compromise with secular doctrines, the non-Christian religions gained a foothold, especially in the northern states. Preceding the Civil War, which began in 1861, Calvinism gradually came to be isolated in the South while Unitarianism, Arminianism, and transcendentalism abounded in the North. Opposites in spirituality do not attract but repel one another. When brought together there are crisis and conflict.

Because of the confusion and crisis of the growing divisiveness, the freedoms guaranteed by the Constitution began crumbling. The Constitution, once worshipped, was now the focus of vehement rhetorical attack. The most prolific and indignant criticism ever made of the Constitution was made by the abolitionists. While the majority of the nation was enthralled in "Constitution worship," the abolitionists, a synonym for revolutionaries, were calling the "sacred" document a "covenant with death" and "an agreement with hell."[10]

The abolitionists, while utilizing the slave issue as a base, had a more fundamental motive than the slavery issue for attacking the South. "Indeed, an important aspect of the Civil War was the Unitarian statist drive for an assault on its Calvinistic enemy, the South ... the anti-Christian, Jacobin attack on slavery had to be fought, and slavery defended, because the revolutionary reordering of society would be far worse than anything it sought to supplant."[11]

The Unitarians had gained a strong foothold in the theological minds of the North. Being anti-Christian in denying the deity of Christ and rejecting the Christian doctrine of the Trinity, the Unitarian-abolitionist drive was fundamentally a move against its spiritual enemy, Calvinism.

With ardent fervor, the Unitarian and transcendentalist forces sought a centralized government which they believed was essential to the erection of the "kingdom of God on earth." In the spirit of Robespierre, the fallen architect of the French Revolution, the Unitarian-abolitionist movement believed that a utopia could be built by human hands.

Julia Ward Howe incorporated her Unitarian faith into such songs as "John Brown's Body" and "The Battle Hymn of the Republic." The latter begins, "Mine eyes have seen the glory of the coming of the Lord." The Lord was portrayed as heroic defender of the Union armies, whereas "the Confederacy is a serpent, which God's Hero must slay, and in proportion to the punishment inflicted by this Hero on God's enemies, who are also His own, the Deity will reward the Hero."[12]

John Brown justified his aggressions upon the South with biblical terms, albeit not without deviating from the original intent of the words. For example, Edmund Wilson's *Patriotic Gore* quoted him as saying: "Without the shedding of blood, there is no remission of sins." Before the war ended, both sides had bled profusely. The South with its emphasis on states' rights and the legality of the Constitution was a stumblingblock to the abolitionist drive. The leaders of the South and the Democrats in the North opposed the abolitionist movement, not because of slavery per se "but because of the philosophy and theology which it represented and because they clearly saw that if this radicalism were to gain supremacy in the national government then there must certainly come in its wake a radical political and social program which would threaten the established order and constitutional government for the nation as a whole."[13]

The Separation Illusion

In order for man to survive he must have a meaningful relationship with God. Even the unregenerate man can prosper if he has Christian presuppositions as his foundation.

The same holds true for a nation. The people whose God is the Lord have a blessed nation. However, "where there is no guidance, the people will fall" (Proverbs 11:14).

The Proverbs declare that fear, or a healthy respect for God, is essential for man to have wisdom. Likewise, "knowledge of the Holy One is understanding" (Proverbs 9:10). The man who denies God and willfully flouts the Scriptures has neither wisdom nor understanding.

Before the Civil War the illusion of separation was ripping at the seams of a country once Christian. The seams were finally sundered and the evil of war burst forth. When God at last stanched the flow, Americans found themselves living in a different nation, a nation enveloped by godless sentiments of hate and revenge, a land to which the Founding Fathers would have found themselves strangers.

Pawns in the Game

Eradicating slavery in the South by giving the black man freedom actually solved little. A great Negro leader stated after the war that the freed man was "free from the individual master but a slave of society."[14] The black man had been freed from the old plantation with nothing but the dusty road beneath his feet.[15]

A generation later, the pattern of change became obvious. Slavery had been replaced by a new caste system in the South—the first of its type to rise on such a large scale since the one born in India some three thousand years before.[16]

The freed man's expectation of equality soon became a wasted dream. The American white man still claimed superiority. "So far conflict between the widely different human races has produced either slavery, caste or miscegenation."[17] Having destroyed the first and third alternatives, the American North as well as the South soon erected the barriers of the second "solution."

Northern radicals were much too involved in destroying the southern aristocracy and way of life to effectuate rehabilitation of the Negro. Instead of receiving an education and financial security, the Negro gained what must have then seemed to be "meaningless political rights."[18]

The triumphant northern system of capitalism persuaded the new centralized federal government to grant forty million acres to one gigantic railroad, but it was unwilling to grant ten million acres to the landless, freed black men of the South.[19]

Slavery in the South was a shameful situation, but the caste system that developed following the Civil War was even more shameful. Slavery was an issue utilized by the northern radicals to destroy the South and in the end, as Bob Dylan has observed, the black man was "only a pawn in their game."[20]

The Flames of Hate

Following the Civil War, a radical Congress assumed control of the government. Viewing the South as a defeated enemy, Congress sought to punish the enemy for its rebellion.

Before his assassination, Abraham Lincoln favored allowing the South to return to the Union without coercion. In the same vein his successor, Andrew Johnson, carried out Lincoln's plan of easing the South back into the Union.

The spark that spread the flames of hate was the rejection of the Fourteenth Amendment by the South. This amendment was written and submitted to the state legislatures for ratification in the summer of 1866.

Understanding the Fourteenth Amendment is necessary because the Supreme Court has been enabled by utilization of the amendment to nationalize the Bill of Rights. Such usage shows how, instead of being a restriction on the federal government, the Bill of Rights has become a tool for furthering centralization of all governmental power in Washington, D.C.

Orville Browning, a senator from Illinois and a member of Andrew Johnson's cabinet, saw the danger in this amendment. He said, "Be assured that if this new provision be engrafted in the Constitution, it will, in time, change the entire structure and texture of our government, and sweep away all the guarantees of safety devised and provided by our patriotic sires of the Revolution."

The Congress that proposed the Fourteenth Amendment was a "rump" Congress because the ten southern states were denied representation—their senators were not allowed into the House or Senate. This exclusion was a violation of Article V of the Constitution, which requires that "no state, without its consent, shall be deprived of equal suffrage in the Senate." It was also a violation of Article I, Section 2, which requires each state to have at least one representative in Congress.

It is apparent that if the southern states had been represented in Congress there would have been no Fourteenth Amendment. It would have been nearly impossible, particularly in the Senate, to gain the necessary two-thirds vote required by Article V for submission of an amendment for ratification to the states.

The southern states as of 1866 had established their own legislatures and governments. The radical Congress, pursuant to the Constitution, submitted the Fourteenth Amendment to the ousted state legislatures for ratification thereby recognizing the *validity* and legality of those legislatures. In fact, these southern legislatures had previously participated in ratification of the Thirteenth Amendment (abolishing slavery). They had also received "presidential recognition."[21]

The ten southern states promptly rejected the amendment, as did California, Kentucky, Maryland, and Delaware. The amendment fell five votes short of ratification.

At the Point of the Bayonet

The libertine Congress reacted to this affront to their dignity by passing the Reconstruction Act on March 2, 1867. The act placed the southern states under military rule with military districts presided over by a military officer appointed by President Andrew Johnson. All civilian authorities were placed under the foreign and dominant authority of the military government. The act completely deprived southern states of all their powers of government and autonomy until such time as Congress would recognize a reorganized government. State autonomy, if any remained, was eradicated.

Referred to as "rebel states," the South was treated as a defeated enemy. This was "an opinion of doubtful legal validity, for the Supreme Court eventually ruled in 1869 that there had been no legal secession at all since the Constitution was, in law, indissoluble."[22] In other words, there was no provision in the Constitution for secession. Therefore, legally the South could not be a defeated enemy since the Union was never dissolved.

The act opened by stating that "no legal state government" existed in the southern states. This is obviously contradictory since, as just discussed, the libertine Congress had already recognized the legislatures of the so-called rebel states by submitting both the Thirteenth and the Fourteenth Amendments to these states for ratification. Contradictory or not, power was in the hands of this radical Congress, which was utilizing it to alter the American form of government. In the space of but a few years the federal government gained immense control as all power became centralized in it. The northern drive for a large national government was successful.

Section 3 of the Reconstruction Act deserves special attention. It required each excluded state of "the southern ten" to ratify the Fourteenth Amendment in order that each might again enjoy the status and rights of a state (including representation in Congress). The states were to remain under military authority until they complied with ratification, among other things. During floor debate on the act, Senator Doolittle of Wisconsin said: "The people of the South have rejected the constitutional amendment, and therefore we will march upon them and force them to adopt it at the point of the bayonet, and establish military power over them until they do adopt it."[23]

Obviously, it was never the intent of the framers of the Constitution that ratification of an amendment be obtained "at the point of the bayonet." Not only was ratification of the Fourteenth Amendment procured through coercion, but it was ratified illegally. President Andrew Johnson, who had tried more than once to restrain the radical Congress, vetoed the act, cited its unconstitutionality and called it "a bill of attainder against nine million people at once." A bill of attainder is a legislative act directed against a person pronouncing him guilty of a capital offense without affording him a trial or conviction according to law. Congress passed the act, however, over the President's veto.

Changing of the Guard

In the meantime, the southern whites were removed from office and denied the right to vote. As a result, virtually every new southern legislature became predominantly black. For example, there were seven whites and ninety-four blacks in the lower House of South Carolina at one time.[24]

It is recognized that the freed black man had a right to representation equal to any other citizen. Unfortunately, the black man had been a slave for centuries and thereby lacked education and experience in government. Because of this, the black governments quickly fell prey to men like Henry Clay Warmoth from Illinois. Expelled from the Union army for theft, Warmoth was later indicted in Texas for stealing cotton.[25] In his campaign for governor of Louisiana he promised the black voters that he would invent a machine that would pump the blood from the black man's veins and replace it with the blood of a white man.[26] He was elected.

Corruption set in, and the puppet governments were infiltrated by the scalawags and the carpetbaggers. The word *scalawag* was coined by the southern Democrats and applied to native southern whites who had become converted Republicans for profit and gain. The carpetbaggers were adventurers who had infested the South from the outside for political and economic gain following the war. Both groups utilized government as the way to quick wealth.

After a decade of military rule, the puppet governments were overturned as the southern states regained control of their legislatures. This time, however, the federal government had established its power to intervene in state politics, thereby dissolving state autonomy.

Too Late for Praying

Eventually, the growing power of northern money began dictating the economic and financial terms of southern reconstruction—a power that generations of Southerners had feared.[27] The South now had no influence in Washington and no way to fight back. The West also came under the domination of northern money. Short of capital, the West gradually became less an ally of the North than an economic satellite.[28]

The ruling Republican party, a mouthpiece of "big business," maintained high tariffs, subsidized the private railroads at the expense of the nation, "curbed" the American labor force by encouraging massive immigration, and centralized the money power in Wall Street, thereby maintaining "a hard-money policy disastrous to the debt-ridden South and West."[29]

Big business could virtually do as it pleased. In Riencourt's words, "[Big business] was the real winner of the Civil War."[30] Northern monopolies began to flourish. Rockefeller justified his industrial monopoly by appeal to Darwin's *Origin of the Species:* "The growth of a large business is merely a survival of the fittest." Andrew Carnegie in the same vein remarked concerning his conversion to Darwinism: "Light came as in a flood and all was clear. Not only had I got rid of theology and the supernatural, but I had found the truth of evolution."[31]

Calvinism was now nearly extinct, and humanistic man no longer was Unitarian or transcendentalist but receded farther into illusion and became an evolutionist. He had found a way to separate himself even farther from God.

The shift was now near completion. The final touches would be added by the Supreme Court some years thereafter by its interpretation of the Fourteenth Amendment. Phase one of the lie had been brought to an end, and the country was now ripe for phase two. America had become post-America. State lines, once rigid and stable, now grew dim under the oppression of a strange and foreign government in Washington. Some in the South called for prayer, but most knew that it was "too late for prayin'."[32]

Altering the Refuge of Lies

The Fourteenth Amendment was intended to have two principal effects. The first was to eradicate Justice Taney's *Dred Scott* decision banning citizenship for the Negro. Section 1 provided citizenship for all persons born or naturalized in this country. "In addition, the intent was to make it illegal for the states to deny equal civil rights to those thus made citizens by the provision that no state was to 'deprive any person of life, liberty, or property, without due process of law' or to 'deny to any person within its jurisdiction the equal protection of the laws.' These two clauses . . . were completely to transform the American constitutional system."[33]

But the transformation has been accomplished by misinterpretation and illusion. As discussed previously, the Bill of Rights (the first ten amendments) was drafted by the framers as limitations on the federal government only. It had no application to the states at all. In fact, in 1833 Chief Justice John Marshall in the *Barron* decision emphasized that the Bill of Rights restricted only the federal government.[34]

With the Warren Court's utilization of Section 1 of the Fourteenth Amendment, the Bill of Rights has come to apply to the states, thereby imposing on them the restrictions meant originally for the federal government. This restatement may seem overly repetitious, but crucial issues that have been ignored for decades bear repeating.

It must be remembered that this amendment, in addition to the Thirteenth and Fifteenth, was written by a radical Congress that was influenced by the abolitionists, who believed that the Constitution was an "agreement with hell." Accordingly, this particular section was written with the intention of at least partially altering that "refuge of lies," the United States Constitution.

The Fourteenth Amendment was drafted to ensure that the freed black man would possess political and civil freedom within the South. Even with forced ratification it did little to further those rights until the early 1950s.

The Grand Fourteenth

Section 1 of the Fourteenth Amendment contains four phrases. The second and third concern us here:

> *No state shall make or enforce any law which shall abridge the privileges and immunities of citizens of the*

United States; nor shall any state deprive any person of
life, liberty, or property, without due process of law.

Section 1 was written in 1866 by James A. Bingham, a representative from Ohio. Bingham was a member of the Joint Committee on Reconstruction, which was chosen by the radical Republicans over the protest of the Democrats to produce a plan of reconstruction. Instead of producing this plan, however, they came forth
with legislation to promote their theory that the government should
be more centralized in order to control the southern states, thereby
democratizing the nation.

Before the Civil War, the country was administered by a constitutional form of government which emphasized state and local
government rather than national control and intervention. The
word *constitution* literally means "constituents," or varying de-
grees and types of government within a scheme of government. For
example, before the Civil War there were local, state, and federal
governments, with emphasis on the local and state government.
There had been very little interference from Washington with the
personal and property rights of the individual up to and including
the Civil War. The three postbellum amendments proposed by the
Joint Committee ended the constitutional form of government and
substituted a national government octopean in nature.

The Joint Committee met in secrecy to promulgate its plans.
The members were so tightlipped that during the debate over the
Fourteenth Amendment one senator stated that the "committee
came to be known in the country as the 'revolutionary tribunal,'
the 'directory,' and the 'star chamber.' "[35] The star chamber was
an English court that became so tyrannical it had to be abolished.
In fact, the constitutionality of the Joint Committee's acts was in
continual question throughout the debates.

The issue to keep in mind is that the Bill of Rights was
"nationalized" and thus became a restriction on the states,
whereas before it restricted the federal government only.

The Supreme Court states that historically Section 1 of the
Fourteenth Amendment was written with the intention to make the
Bill of Rights applicable to the states. After careful study it be-
comes clear that this is an erroneous assumption.

The Forked Tongue

John Bingham, author of controversial Section 1, was a member of the radical Republicans, who dominated Congress during the years immediately following the Civil War. Section 1 was rejected by the South (and four other states) not only because of its grants to the black man and its democratic leveling of all men, but also because of the change it would bring about in the nature of the government.

From the beginning, Bingham's wording in Section 1 was a problem. The "privileges and immunities" clause declares: "No state shall make or enforce any law which shall abridge the privileges or immunities of citizens of the United States."

In the 1866 debates on the passage of the Fourteenth Amendment, Bingham specifically stated that this amendment did not change the Constitution.[36] In fact, he copied this phrase from Article IV, Section 2 of the Constitution itself. However, in 1871, in a debate in Congress, he contradicted himself by stating that this amendment protected "the rights of citizens against states, and individuals in states, *never* before granted."[37] Some members of Congress were astonished at this statement and indicated they wouldn't have voted for the amendment if this had been made known.

In the 1866 debates concerning the Fourteenth Amendment Bingham *never* once stated that the amendment transferred the restrictions placed on the federal government by the Bill of Rights to the state governments. In 1866, however, he was more concerned with the true intention of Section 1 as well as the entire Fourteenth Amendment, which gave Congress the power to act to prohibit the states from passing legislation to interfere with the civil rights of the blacks. Five years after the amendment had been ratified and was law, he asserted that the "privileges and immunities" clause now meant that the restrictions in the Bill of Rights should apply to the states.[38] Since the Fourteenth Amendment was focused on the states, he argued that the first ten amendments to the Constitution (the Bill of Rights) were prohibitions that bound the states as well as the general or federal government.

It is important to note that Bingham specifically stated that the "privileges and immunities" clause incorporates the Bill of Rights into, or applies it to, the state governments.

In 1873 the Supreme Court had its first opportunity to pass on Section 1—at issue was the privileges-and-immunities clause. As Professor Edward S. Corwin put it, "The privileges-and-immunities clause ... enjoys the distinction of having been rendered a 'practical nullity' by a single decision of the Supreme Court rendered within five years after its ratification."[39] The Court held that since this clause specifically refers to "citizens of the United States," it protects only federal rights and has nothing to do with those persons holding individual state citizenship. This may seem to be splitting hairs, but the Court holds the wording of Section 1 to exactly what it states and nothing more.[40]

The Court here is protecting states' rights, but is also at the same time refuting Bingham's argument that this clause somehow makes the Bill of Rights applicable to the states. This decision in effect sweeps away the privileges-and-immunities clause. However, this clause was the heart of Bingham's argument concerning the Bill of Rights. To say the least, Bingham's illusionary bubble burst.

The states' autonomy, although pale, was now destined to be strangled by the due process clause of Section 1.

Due Process of Law

Bingham borrowed the due-process clause from the Fifth Amendment. As rendered in the Fourteenth it reads: "[No] state [shall] deprive any person of life, liberty, or property, without due process of law...." The amendment presents a problem by failing to define the meaning of "due process." It contains no description of those processes which it was intended to allow or forbid. The highly esteemed Justice Frankfurter, in the *Adamson* decision (1947), stated most affirmatively that because the due-process clause is "not authoritatively formulated" in the Constitution, this does not give judges a license to make it anything they want.[41] Unfortunately, his admonition was ignored.

Justice Hugo Black, a former member of the Ku Klux Klan who has been caricatured as the Warren Court's John the Baptist, dissented in *Adamson*. He asserted that Section 1 of the Fourteenth Amendment nationalized the Bill of Rights (making it applicable to the states), a position which smoothed the way for the Warren Court.[42]

It was Black's belief that the due-process clause of Section 1 absorbed the Bill of Rights, thereby transferring its restrictions to the states. He claimed that his "study of the historical events that culminated in the Fourteenth Amendment" supported his view. He either had misread history or was deliberately promulgating a doctrine whose consequences he did not fully foresee. As illustrated above, Bingham, the author of Section 1, stated himself that it was the privileges-and-immunities clause and not the due-process clause that absorbed the Bill of Rights. Bingham's statement, made five years after ratification of the amendment, was heavily criticized by his contemporaries and was eventually discredited by the Supreme Court in 1873.

It was Black's influence that swung the Warren Court and allowed the federal government to stretch its tentacles into the state domain. In other words, and I emphasize this fact, the Supreme Court of the Warren era (1953–1969) in this particular instance has "made up" law out of nothing. The Warren Court ignored history in order to accomplish its objectives. This is not only unethical and illegal, but also an attempt to perpetuate illusion. The Court, on a case by case basis, applied most of the restrictions of the Bill of Rights to the states.

Move into Totalitarianism

Laissez-faire ("hands off") was the ideal grasped so firmly by the framers of the Constitution. The fear of big government gave rise to the first ten amendments (the Bill of Rights). The Supreme Court by ignoring history and by employing the due-process clause to nationalize the Bill of Rights has accomplished just the opposite of what was intended by the framers. What was intended as a restriction on the federal government (the Bill of Rights) is now a cluster of restrictions on the states.

The Warren Court interpreted the "due process" clause so as to invoke the restrictions of the Bill of Rights onto the states in direct contradiction to the original intent of the framers of the amendments. At first the Court was selective in its incorporation and absorption of the Bill of Rights through the due process clause. However, before Chief Justice Earl Warren had "resigned in 1969 the Court had almost totally 'absorbed' the Bill of Rights in the Fourteenth Amendment."[43]

How can this be? How can the framers' intent be denied? By the process of liberal, relativistic interpretation the Court has taken the word "liberty" found in the due process clause to refer to the "freedoms" of the Bill of Rights. Since the Fourteenth reads, "No State shall ... deprive any person of ... liberty ...", the Court holds that this alters the meaning of the Bill of Rights so that it now is a prohibition on the states. This is at best an ambiguous attempt at legal semantics juggling. This sleight of hand way of interpretation has nurtured a radical shift in constitutional theory. It has been the springboard that has caused the shift from a constitutional form of government to a centralized form of government.

The shift has occurred as illustrated below:

I. *In the Beginning*
1791
Bill of Rights
originally was
restriction on
federal government.

Federal Government

Bill of Rights

State Governments

Bill of Rights
served as a wall
of separation
between the two
forms of government.

II. *The Shift*
   1976
   Bill of Rights now
   interpreted as re-
   strictions on the
   state governments
   by way of the
   Fourteenth Amendment
   "due process" clause.

Federal Government

The wall of separation
disappears into the
"due process" clause.

State Governments

   As a result of the shift, the country, through a strange trans-
mogrification, has developed from a federation of constituent states
and local governments to a highly centralized, octopean, bureaucratic system. It is no longer America, but post-America. The
Constitution, once worshipped as a treasury of freedoms, is now an
instrument utilized to build a godlike government. In consequence,
the totalitarian state stands beckoning for its curtain call, and Orwell's *1984* becomes more of a reality moment by moment.

₹ 4 ₹

Primal Antichrist

*Children, it is the last hour; and just as you heard
that antichrist is coming, even now many antichrists
have arisen; from this we know that it is the last hour.*

I John 2:18 (ca. A.D. 90)

Approximately A.D. 65 the apostle Peter issued a stern warning
to his fellow Christians to be "of sober spirit, be on the alert" for
"your adversary, the devil, prowls about like a roaring lion, seeking someone to devour" (I Peter 5:8).

During the presidency and later years of Thomas Jefferson,
many Christians set themselves against the Virginian with only a
little less vigor than they would against Satan himself. In fact, before his presidency ended someone designated him the "antichrist."[1] Even Jefferson's political foes in the press and pulpit
labeled him an "atheist and infidel" on numerous occasions.

To many in our day these titles would constitute honor, incur-
ring little indignation from the recipient. To Jefferson these charges
were insults to his dignity, calling for retaliation.

The following analyses of Jefferson's beliefs and statements on
the church and religion are not wholly complimentary. Although a
brilliant man, he also had failings. Some may still look upon criticism of American heroes as bordering on blasphemy, but the tenor
of our times definitely does not call for false hero worship.

Several years ago an acquaintance of mine, who was an ardent
follower of seer Edgar Cayce, told me Thomas Jefferson had been
reincarnated and was at that time a disgruntled bus driver in Brook-
lyn. No matter how ridiculous this may seem, he truly believed it.

The late Supreme Court justice, Hugo Black, would not have believed this. He did, however, believe that Jefferson's words were but little short of revelations from above. Bereft of the Scriptures to guide one's life, a man is prone to believe anything.

The apotheosis of Jefferson has caused problems. The utilization of his writings by the Supreme Court in handing down decisions has created an even more perplexing situation. The ballyhoo given certain statements of Jefferson while ignoring other pronouncements by him concerning religion has placed a dark shroud over the meaning of the First Amendment to the United States Constitution.

Jefferson on Jesus and Religion

In 1797 Jefferson met the well-known Unitarian Joseph Priestly, who became his religious adviser.[2] Jefferson thereupon adopted Priestly's "reasonable Christian" approach to religion. To Jefferson this meant establishing a self-made religion by rationalizing away those sections of the Bible that were not pleasing to him.

In the winter of 1804-1805, while serving as President of the United States, Jefferson began the chore of writing his own private New Testament. He saw the task as one of removing all references to the supernatural contained in the Scriptures—the virgin birth of Christ, His resurrection, the miracles, etc.—replacing them with his own interpretation of what took place during Christ's ministry.[3]

In 1816 his compilation was completed. The work was entitled "Morals of Jesus." In the end, however, he kept the entire work a secret for fear of fueling the flames of the criticism he had already received from his Christian enemies.[4] Following his death, it was published under the title Jefferson's Bible.

Jefferson's hatred of clergymen emerges throughout his writings. His battles with them and the established church, however, never led Jefferson to revoke his belief in the excellent qualities he saw in the life of the man called Jesus.

Jefferson personally admired Jesus Christ the man and His teachings. He felt Jesus' doctrines were simple and tended to bring happiness to man. However, concerning the deity of Christ, Jefferson believed this was one of those "demoralizing dogmas of Calvin."[5] Calvin's doctrines of the Trinity and divine election were erroneous assertions leading Jefferson to conclude that the Calvinists were "the false shepherds [and] usurpers of the Christian name, teaching a counter-religion made up of the deliria of crazy imaginations...."[6] Calvin's faith was to the man from Monticello a religion of demonism, and Calvin himself was "an atheist."

In a word, Jefferson rejected the teachings of Scripture and asserted his own faith. He believed the early nineteenth century would see a revival. Indeed, "the genuine doctrine of one only God is reviving, and I trust that there is not a young man now living in the United States who will not die a Unitarian."[7] Unitarianism and its denial of the deity of Christ did grow to major proportions several years later. This faith didn't pioneer revival, but did lead to a revolutionary shift in the form of government that was to guide toward totalitarianism in the future.

As to his beliefs on religion as a whole, Jefferson was clearly pluralistic. It was his premise that a multiplicity of sects was desirable to guard against tyranny in numbers. Established religion, or, more properly, the state support of a single church, was simply intolerable to him. This was a basic overreaction of his aversion to the established Church of England and Puritan theocracy.

Jefferson and Madison both envisioned the established church, or any type of theocratic institution, as the enemy of freedom. Not so James Russell Lowell. The famous nineteenth-century poet and diplomat said, "Puritanism, believing itself with the seed of religious liberty, laid, without knowing it, the seed of democracy." The foundations of liberty were laid by the very doctrines James Madison and Thomas Jefferson fought against. Their fanaticism led them to extremes; happily, the men who drafted the Constitution did not assume such drastic views.

The Seed of the Illusion

The First Amendment commences with the declaration that "Congress shall make no law respecting an establishment of religion, or prohibiting the free exercise thereof." The First Amendment will be discussed in detail in the following chapters, but it is sufficient to say here that this clause was placed into the Constitution to prohibit the federal government from setting up one national church, thereby interfering with the states' religious preferences.

At one time the Bill of Rights constituted restrictions on the federal government alone and not on the states. As intended by the framers, this amendment would leave the states a free hand in religion—free to establish their churches, free to permit Bible reading and prayer in the schools. The area of religion was purely a state matter.

In 1962 and 1963 with two momentous decisions the Supreme Court declared death to God in the public schools of this country.[8] Nietzsche's nightmarish death wish seemed a reality, and God somehow had become unconstitutional.

The Court ruled that the so-called wall of separation which supposedly stood between church and state, prevented the use of state-directed prayer and Bible reading in the public schools. This utilization of government-directed prayer, the Court declared, was a violation of the establishment-of-religion clause in the First Amendment of the Constitution.

Hugo Black, author of the school-prayer decision, gave the classic interpretation of the First Amendment establishment clause. In a 1947 decision Justice Black said, "In the words of Jefferson, the clause against establishment of religion by law was intended to erect 'a wall of separation between church and state.' "[9]

It is important to recognize that with this one brief statement Jefferson planted the seed of the illusion that was to sprout full bloom in the mid-twentieth century. It was the Supreme Court's, and, individually, Hugo Black's, capitalization on Jefferson's statement, however, that raised the wall of illusion to its present-day height.

The Great Wall

As men struggle to be free from God they eventually enslave themselves. Like small children, they draw a line on the earth, audaciously commanding God to stay on His side while they go their own way. That such can be is both an illusion and a lie. No matter how strenuously one labors to hold God back, he will ultimately fail. At this particular point man either despairs and calls on God or falls off the deep end. The deep end is either suicide or pretension. A man can pretend God is not there or he can separate himself from God by erecting an illusionary wall. Either way man lies to himself.

Jefferson, courting illusion, had erected a wall between himself and God. Subsequently, he attempted to erect such a wall between the church and state governments. He used as his authority for this illusion the Constitution. Careful study shows him wrong. The popular phrase *wall of separation,* indicating an impassable gulf between church and state, is nowhere to be found in the United States Constitution. In fact, the term *church and state* is lacking in the First Amendment.

The phrases had their origin in a letter written by Jefferson in 1802 to a group of Baptists in Danbury, Connecticut, in which he maintained that it was the purpose of the First Amendment to build "a wall of separation between church and state."[10] It is not improbable that this statement was motivated by an "impish desire" to hurl a brick at the Congregationalist–Federalist hierarchy of Connecticut, "whose leading members" had earlier denounced him as an "infidel" and "atheist."[11]

The deceptive motivation behind Jefferson's wall-of-separation statement did not really emerge until 1805, when in his Second Inaugural Address he stated, "In matters of religion I have considered that its free exercise is placed by the Constitution independent of the powers of the General Government. I have therefore undertaken on no occasion to prescribe the religious exercises suited to it, but have left them, as the Constitution found them, under the direction and discipline of the church or state authorities acknowledged by the several religious societies." Obviously, Jefferson had in three years rethought his statement made to the Baptists, to wit, that the purpose of the First Amendment was to erect "a wall of separation between church and state." Jefferson, in his second statement on religion, brings his view in line with the Constitution, which erects a wall between the federal government and the state government on matters of religion.

First of all, many of the men who drafted the Constitution were Christians, and the rest at least lived lives based on Christian presuppositions and biblical principles. Their main concern with the First Amendment religion clause was in preventing the federal government from establishing a national church and, in conjunction therewith, protecting their own state-established churches or state-preferred Christian denominations. At the time of the ratification of the First Amendment in 1791, over one-third of the thirteen colonies had established churches, which fact meant that many of the states were supporting a single church or religion. The First Amendment states that "Congress shall make no law respecting an establishment of religion, or prohibiting the free exercise thereof." The word *Congress* has from the beginning been interpreted to mean the federal government. *Respecting* is literally defined as "having anything to do with." And *establishment* has historically meant "government support of a single church or government preference of one Christian creed or denomination over another." Therefore, modernizing the language of the First Amendment, it would read like this today, "The federal government shall make no law having anything to do with supporting a single church, or prohibiting the free exercise of religion by the states." As you can very well see, if this amendment is not viewed in its historical context, then it can become distorted. That is exactly the error committed by the Supreme Court in its interpretation of the First Amendment.

Let us now return to Jefferson's statement. Initially, he said that the first Amendment's purpose was to build "a wall of separation between church and state." Taking this statement for what it's worth, the situation would look like this:

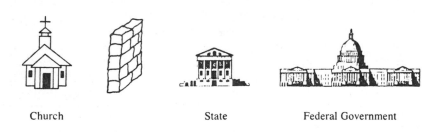

Church   State   Federal Government

In the 1802 statement he supposedly places a wall of separation between the church on the one side, and the federal and state governments on the other.

However, in his 1805 statement Jefferson places the great wall between the federal government and the state governments, as illustrated below:

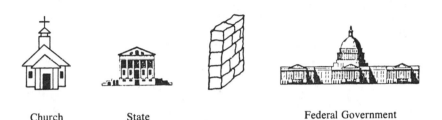

Church   State   Federal Government

Jefferson specifically stated following his Second Inaugural Address that "religion ... is ... independent of the powers of the General [or federal] Government ... and that religious exercises should be left ... as the Constitution found them, under the direction and discipline of the church or state authorities." Constitutional law authority Edward S. Corwin competently summed up Jefferson's 1805 statement: "In short, the principal importance of the amendment lay in the separation which it effected between the respective jurisdictions of state and nation regarding religion, rather than in its bearing on the question of the separation of church and state."[12] The purpose of the First Amendment was "to exclude from the national government all power to act on the subject ... of religion."[13] The First Amendment, therefore, provides freedom *for* religion, not *from* religion. The states by this amendment were afforded that freedom in the area of religion.

Indeed, the federal government was not even given the power to guarantee religious freedom in the Constitution. Moreover,

Madison himself, during the debates concerning the adoption of the First Amendment, asserted that there "is not a shadow of right in the general government to intermeddle with religion. Its least interference with it would be a most flagrant usurpation."[14]

It becomes readily apparent that when the great wall, which the Supreme Court so staunchly insists is a barrier between church and state, is brought to the light it is nonexistent. Amazingly, as early as 1879 the Supreme Court had declared that Jefferson's wall-of-separation phrase was "almost an authoritative declaration of the scope and effect of the Amendment."[15]

The striking fact about the Supreme Court's claim concerning the First Amendment, and the utilization of Jefferson's wall of separation as the authority, is that Thomas Jefferson had nothing to do with the writing of our Constitution. Jefferson was in Paris in 1791, when the First Amendment was written. Even Jefferson's own language does not support the view that the First Amendment allows the Court to strike state-directed religious exercises from public schools. The Court, by relying on historically inaccurate information, has erased three hundred years of American tradition and has in the process violated the very law it was sworn to uphold.

In the Dream

Truth was the goal of the so-called Golden Age of Greece. Truth in our age, though, has become as elusive as the fugitive from justice. "Pop poet" Bob Dylan, with more scruples than most pulpit priests, said:

> I know no answers and no truth
> For absolutely no soul alive.
> I will listen to no one
> Who tells me morals.
> There are no morals
> And I dream a lot.[16]

How can the United States Supreme Court deny the historical meaning behind the Constitution? The answer has already been provided by one of the Court's bygone prophets. Chief Justice Vinson of the Supreme Court, shortly after World War II, was quoted as saying, "Nothing is more certain in modern society than the principle that there are no absolutes."[17] This is the modern humanistic, relativistic philosophy, which holds as its basis that nothing is positively the same every time. Everything is subject to change, depending on the particular circumstances. What is bad in one instance can be declared good next time around. It merely depends on the situation. All is relative.

This philosophy is a direct denial of Scriptural truth. It is also a contradiction of the foundations upon which the Constitution was based. The Constitution was written on the Christian presupposition of absolutes and antithesis. Antithesis holds that A cannot be non-A. If something is good, then it cannot be bad; or if something is an establishment of religion (meaning governmental support of a single church), then something else is not (a twenty-two-word prayer). Bob Dylan is wrong. There is truth.

By utilizing this relativistic philosophy in its decisions, the Supreme Court has taken the First Amendment, written to prevent the federal government from interfering with the state religious establishments, and twisted its meaning so that now the federal government dictates to the states where and when they may pray. What the First Amendment was intended to prevent is now being accomplished by process of the First Amendment. This is relativism. And the intent of the framers, therefore, is denied all significance.

The Constitution, by being subjected to this type of reasoning, becomes more antiquated with each decision. Interpretation of it by the Court has become as unreliable as blind chance itself. If the Constitution is not being followed, then the United States, in effect, has no constitution.

Legal Illegality

Christianity was the religion of the men who wrote the Constitution. In fact, reaching back in time a few years from the date of the drafting of the Constitution, it is significant to note that two-thirds of the signers of the Declaration of Independence were Episcopalians.[18] Justice Story says it well:

> *Probably at the time of the adoption of the Constitution,*
> *and of the amendment to it . . . the general, if not the uni-*

versal, sentiment in America was that Christianity ought to receive encouragement from the state, so far as was not incompatible with the private rights of conscience and the freedom of religious worship. An attempt to level all religions, and to make it a matter of state policy to hold all in utter indifference, would have created universal disapprobation if not universal indignation.[19]

It is conceded by most that this was once a Christian nation. The Constitution was written to reflect the Christian conscience of America. The First Amendment was to ensure noninterference with the Christian religious freedom of the states. The Supreme Court, by ruling that state-directed prayer and Bible reading in the public schools are unconstitutional, has violated that amendment. The Court, by patent misinterpretation of the Constitution, acted illegally. The appropriate question is: If the very judicial representatives of the government fail to uphold the law, how can they, in turn, expect the citizens to respect the law?

} 5 {

The Battle for
the Schools
Priests Without Prayer

*[Judges have] a peculiar chant and jargon of their
own, that no other mortal can understand, and wherein
all their laws are written, which they take special care
to multiply; whereby they have wholly confounded the
very essence of truth and falsehood.*

Jonathan Swift

*We believe that the cause of theology and morals is
one, and that whatever banishes God from the heart
of things, with the same edict excludes the ideal, the
ethical, from the life of man. Whatever exiles theology
makes ethics an expatriate.*

John Dewey

Pray without ceasing.

Apostle Paul

The modernistic mentality cannot understand why some men
speak to the air proclaiming there is a God who listens to them. If
one does not believe in the supernatural, then prayer seems pure
foolishness. Moreover, these modern secularites are outraged when
their children in any way petition the sky for answers.

In 1962 the two opposing sides met on a judicial battlefield, armed with legal semantics. When the last shot was fired, the Christians had lost the battle. The war, however, continues.

A Jealous God

Simply put, prayer is communication between man and God. The New Testament emphasizes the Christian's role in fervent prayer not only for himself but also for other believers and the world situation. Prayer is an essential aspect of Christian living.

The state or government that has proclaimed itself god is jealous of the true God. For any being under state control to petition an entity other than the state is seen as an attempt to deny its authority as a deity. The state's religion, being the religion of humanity, cannot tolerate foreign religious practices within its domain. *As it was when Christ was on earth*

The statist lawgiver, the United States Supreme Court, has determined that this type of Christian religious activity should not be permitted. Although the Court's language may be couched in flaccid terms, the impact of the decisions has been extremely damaging. Suffice it to say that prayer has all but been eliminated from the public schools as a result of the prayer cases.

The Statist Tabernacle

The early church not only served as a place of prayer and singing but was a teaching institution as well. The Word of God was strongly preached in order to utilize the knowledge gained as a weapon for the glory of God.

As the Christian church has decayed and abandoned this teaching approach, the public schools have assumed the role of the teacher of knowledge. The knowledge taught is presented from the secular viewpoint, thereby denying the Scriptures any worth in this process.

The public schools function as the church for the religion of humanity, promoting the statist faith. Their philosophy is that man is good, and as he evolves into eternity he will perfect himself. This teaching is directly opposed to the Christian belief that man is a sinner and the only way he can become perfect, or mature, is to accept the atoning sacrifice made by Jesus Christ.

The priests of this culture are the educators and teachers who themselves profess godly revelation and wisdom. They teach the faith handed down by their god. To them it is truth, and whatever conflicts with this truth is invalid. Prayer to the Christian God is taboo, for these priests see no need for prayer.

The Scriptures state that for a man to possess wisdom and understanding he must reverence the true God as well as have a saving knowledge of Him (Proverbs 9:10). The non-Christian teacher, therefore, has neither wisdom nor understanding, and without these two essential traits he cannot be a teacher in the true sense of the word.

One does not have to look far to see that the public schools are satanic imitations of the true God's institutional church. And in true imitation they preach statist faith with the zeal once exhibited by the Christian church.

The true failure admitted by theologians for years has been within the church of God itself. The church has allowed the government to chip away at its faith and function until it has been reduced to the lowest depths in history. To this type of church Christ so relevantly spoke, "I know your deeds, that you are neither cold nor hot. So because you are lukewarm, and neither hot nor cold, I will vomit you out of my mouth" (Revelation 3:15-16). It is neither presumptuous nor inept to conclude that the church of this day is so deserving of this judgment.

The Continuing Race War

The Christians are a spiritual race chosen to serve as the sons of God (I Peter 2:9). The other spiritual race is also an appointed race, but doom happens to be their lot (I Peter 2:8). One is either a child of the Light or a child of the darkness. This delineation is clearly portrayed in the Scriptures.

The conflict between the light and the darkness is inevitable. It occurs daily. Battle after battle is fought, but the war trudges onward toward the grand finale depicted in the book of Revelation.

The race war is evident in the cases that have been concerned with the subtle disestablishment of the Christian church. For instance, in the New York prayer case, the atheists, the American Jewish Committee and the Synagogue Council of America were in coalition together to eradicate a short denominational prayer from being recited in the New York public schools.

Why the continuous hassle from the other side in these cases? The Scriptures as always provide the answer. Christ said, ". . . the light is come into the world, and men loved the darkness rather than the light; for their deeds were evil" (John 3:19). The Scriptures and prayer project the light onto the deeds of men and instead of confessing their evil they run to hide in the darkness. In order to snuff the light, the sons of darkness believed that cutting the reciting of prayer from school would aid in their gaining control of the system.

Darkness has indeed fallen on the public schools. Many schools will not allow prayer, Scripture reading, or even the mention of the word God within their walls. However, administrators are crying out, "The children are out of hand. The kids have lost any concept of morality." In the words of John Dewey, who ardently promoted statist education, "the cause of theology and morals is one."

A battle was won but not the war. To the victor go the spoils.

Early Offensive

When the governmental power was centralized in Washington, D.C. following the Civil War, the move to make the state the final arbitrator became entrenched. Slowly but surely the state began asserting its authority over the church. Disestablishment had begun, making way for the new religion.

The first bite from the apple came in 1878 in the Supreme Court decision *Reynolds* v. *United States*.[1] The accused in this case asserted the right to practice polygamy which he claimed was a tenet of his religion, Mormonism. He pleaded that the penalty for failure to practice polygamy would result in "damnation in the life to come."[2]

Congress, in an attempt to restrict such practices, had passed a law making bigamy a crime in any territory under the jurisdiction or control of the United States. The Supreme Court upheld the legislation, stating that laws are made for the control of actions, "and while they cannot interfere with mere religious belief and opinions, they may with practices."[3] The Court went on to point out that if such practices were permitted this would "make the professed doctrines of religious belief superior to the law of the land, and in effect ... permit every citizen to become a law unto himself. Government could exist only in name under such circumstances."[4]

Although the Court here is correct in some of its propositions, it is extremely important to recognize that religious freedom was reduced to "mere belief and opinions." The practice of religion externally was therefore subject to restriction and eradication by the government.

Religion was now embroiled in a belief–action dichotomy. The First Amendment embraces two concepts—the freedom to believe and the freedom to act. The first is absolute, the Court held, but the second remains subject to regulation for the so-called protection of society.

What the Court succeeded in doing was rendering the freedom of religion of the First Amendment practically worthless. For as the old common-law wisdom held, the devil himself knows not the thoughts of man.

The Court in this case erroneously utilized Jefferson's wall-of-separation statement made to the Danbury Baptists in 1802 as an authoritative arbiter of the purpose of the First Amendment. As pointed out earlier, Jefferson retracted this statement in his Second Inaugural Address in 1805. The Court, therefore, labored under a misconception in using this as one of the bases of its decision.

The Court and the country were yet working off the foundation of Christian presuppositions. Moreover, the Court presupposed that the existing religious structure was Christian in character. It saw the Mormon practice of polygamy as contrary to Christian ethics. The Court, therefore, was forced to deny this religious practice.

"Implicit in the court's decision was the equation of Christian moral standards with civilization. The legal structure they defended was implicitly Christian. It is *other* religions which are restricted to 'mere opinion' when they are in conflict with the religious establishment...."[5] It follows from this that if the state assumes a new religion, those religions that are in conflict with the state religion will be restricted to "mere belief and opinions."

The danger in the decision lies in the groundwork it laid for the disestablishment of the Christian church. The state always functions on the foundation of some religion. Its laws are always religious in origin.[6] "Law is the expression of the will of a god, it is formulated by the priest, it is given religious sanction, it is accompanied by magic ritual."[7]

Laws also manifest the morality of the religion of the state; they are propositional evidence of what it believes to be good or bad. In this way, laws become a tool of warfare against foreign religions with a different set of moral codes. If the foreign religion will not succumb to the authority of the state, then it must be eliminated by disestablishment and reduced to mental speculation.

The secular laws of today are based not on Christian precepts, as laws in this country once were, but on the religion of humanity. It should come as no surprise then that practices in the state domain, such as public schools, are restricted and reduced to mere opinion only.

The New York Prayer Case

Some twenty years preceding the prayer decision, in 1940, the Supreme Court reversed history by holding that the First Amendment prohibitions as supposedly altered by the Fourteenth Amendment now applied not only to the federal government but also to the state governments.[8] The Court so interpreted the Fourteenth Amendment as to alter the original meaning of both amendments.

Subsequently, in 1948, the Supreme Court in an opinion written by Hugo Black invalidated a program conducted in the public schools of Champaign, Illinois. These schools permitted a religious teacher or minister to come into their schools and present thirty to forty-five minutes of religious training per week. The Court held that this *practice* violated the First Amendment to the Constitution because it was an establishment of a religion.[9] The decision was only a prelude to what the Court would decide fourteen years later.

In 1962 the State Board of Regents of New York composed a prayer which it recommended to local boards for the purpose of moral and spiritual training. The New York school officials were simply giving expression to what the American people had adhered to for centuries. They were in no way differing from the Founding Fathers, whose faith in God and dependence upon Him penetrated both their public and their private lives. The framers refrained not from mentioning God in public. Nor were they reluctant openly to pray to Him, to set up chaplaincies, and ask the chief of state to call a day of prayer and thanksgiving to God.

The Board of Education of Union Free School District Number 9 of New Hyde Park of New York, by recommendation of the state board, directed its public school districts to recite the following prayer: "Almighty God, we acknowledge our dependence upon Thee, and we beg Thy blessings upon us, our parents, our teachers and our country."[10]

Containing twenty-two words and lasting less than ten seconds, the prayer was recited at the beginning of each school day. Students who did not want to participate in reciting the prayer were either permitted to remain silent or excused from the room while the prayer was recited.

Shortly after the prayer recitation was adopted by the school district, the parents of ten pupils brought suit in the New York Court of Appeals to have the prayer declared in violation of the religion clause of the First Amendment, which clause reads, "Congress shall make no law respecting an establishment of religion. ..." The parents contended that since the "prayer was composed by governmental officials as a part of a governmental program to further religious beliefs," it was an *establishment of religion*.[11] For this reason, the parents asserted, the state's utilization of this prayer breached the so-called wall of separation between church and state.

In *Engel* v. *Vitale,* Justice Hugo Black agreed with the parents that the twenty-two-word prayer was an establishment of religion. In writing the opinion, he stated, " ...the constitutional prohibition against laws respecting an establishment of religion must at least mean that in this country it is no part of the business of government to compose official prayers for any group of the American people to recite as part of a religious program carried on by government." Even if the prayer was denominationally neutral (not favoring one denomination over another) and pupils were not forced to recite the prayer, it was yet, in the words of Hugo Black, an establishment of religion breaching "the constitutional wall of separation between church and state."[12]

As pointed out earlier, Jefferson's 1802 wall-of-separation statement, although given constitutional stature by the Supreme Court, was retracted publicly by Jefferson himself in 1805. He had misinterpreted the First Amendment, and he knew it. The Court, however, ignored history.

Justice Black, in effect, declared that the public domain is out of bounds for God. Public communion with Him now in the public schools was to be prohibited.

A chilling effect of this Supreme Court ruling is not only its attempt to fortify the wall of separation between church and state, but also its attempt to build a secular ceiling preventing public communication between the child and God. The substance of the holding is that the child's thoughts must not openly ascend to the Creator while on public property. This reasoning denies to the child the right audibly to petition his God in emergency.

Forbidding prayer involves, besides the relationship of church and state, the direct relationship between the Almighty and this country. In times of peace spiritual severance may seem of little moment, but in a time of national emergency the country may desire communication with God. The question is: Will He listen?

Madison and the First Amendment

In the process of deciding this case, Hugo Black relied heavily on James Madison's famous *Memorial and Remonstrance Against Religious Assessments*. He utilized this writing to support his view that the First Amendment somehow had erected a wall of separation between the church and the state governments.

Madison's *Remonstrance* was addressed to the Virginia legislature in 1784, over five years before the drafting of the First Amendment. It was in opposition to a bill, then pending, that would have imposed a tax to be used to pay Christian teachers. After Madison's *Remonstrance,* or protest, a vote on the bill was postponed and it died in committee.

Madison's view on religion was that no state could have an established religion (governmental preference of one religion or creed over another, or governmental support of a single church). As many of the states then had established religions (or at least preferred Christianity to other religions), Madison's opinion on the subject was definitely a minority viewpoint.

Justice Black erroneously believed that Madison's views in his *Remonstrance* were controlling when the First Amendment was drafted. Nothing could be further from the truth. Black's reasoning on this subject led constitutional-law authority Ernest J. Brown to comment, "To treat it [the *Remonstrance*] as authoritatively incorporated in the First Amendment is to take grotesque liberties."[13]

Further, Black specifically states that Madison was "the author of the First Amendment."[14] A careful examination of the records of the First Congress of the United States fails to support this contention. In fact, the First Amendment was the product of a special committee of the First Congress. True, Madison, as a member of the First Congress, influenced the drafting in part of the Bill of Rights, "which was to guarantee, forever, the basic liberties, including religious, of all Americans."[15] If the authorship of the First Amendment belongs to anyone, that person is Livermore of New Hampshire. He came closest to the wording of our present amendment when he proposed the following amendment: ". . . Congress shall make no law touching religion, or infringing the rights of conscience."[16]

Moreover, Madison proposed two amendments to the new Constitution which dealt with religion, numbered four and five. His amendment four restricted the federal government in matters of religion and amendment five placed restrictions on the state governments in matters of religion.

The amendment dealing with the states and religion was soundly attacked. Mr. Tucker of South Carolina objected stringently to Madison's amendment five as to state restrictions because his state had an established religion. He said, "It will be much better . . . to leave the state governments to themselves, and not to interfere with them. . . . I therefore move, sir, to strike out these words."[17]

It is important to note at this point that Madison's proposed amendment, having as its motive a special restriction on the states, indicates that without such a restriction the states were free to involve themselves in religious matters. This the states had always done.

Finally, after some deliberation in the First Congress, Madison's proposed amendment five, restricting the states in religious matters, was eliminated. The Senate unequivocally rejected the amendment outright.

Many of the members of the First Congress were Christians, and many of the states had established religions. It would therefore seem that the framers were well aware of what they were doing when they constructed the First Amendment. These men feared the possibility of the federal government having the power to set up a national church or religion that would interfere with their freedom of religion. They certainly couldn't allow Madison's views on state restrictions to prevail.

In sum, Madison cannot validly be appealed to in support of the Court's opinion in the prayer case. Hugo Black, however, did just that. This would seem to leave the *Engel* case with very little merit.

The Puritans

Justice Black evidenced other deficiencies in history during the course of the *Engel* case. He makes an erroneous claim when he states "that a union of government and religion tends to destroy government and to degrade religion."[18] Notice that Black says *"religion,"* not *"church."* Throughout his opinion, he stresses that the union of church and state has a denigrating effect on both.

History reveals that the union of church and state has brought forth some evil, but history does not demonstrate that the union of the state (or government) and the Christian *religion* has produced any harm. One need only read the history of the United States to be convinced of this. England as well as the Scandinavian countries might well offer evidence that "the union of church and state has neither destroyed the governments of their respective countries nor degraded their religion."[19]

Further, Justice Black strains hard to make the church–state struggles a matter of whether or not there was governmentally prescribed prayer. History, however, fails to support such a conclusion.

Black does little better when dealing with Puritan history. Before migration to the American continent, while yet in England, the Puritans never protested governmentally sponsored prayer as Black implies. The Puritans who petitioned the crown to install Christian teachers in the schools certainly would not protest the utilization of governmentally sponsored prayers.

Justice Black finally drops off the deep end when he concludes, "It is a matter of history that this very practice of establishing governmentally composed prayers for religious services was one of the reasons which caused many of our early colonists to leave England and seek religious freedom in America."[20] This is unhistorical and misleading.

Governmentally established prayers were not the bone of contention in England during the sixteenth and seventeenth centuries. Indeed, nothing could be further from the truth. Nor was governmental sponsorship of religion the issue in the "Puritan revolution," as it has been called.[21]

To substantiate his contention, Black gives two references: "See generally Pullman, *The History of the Book of Common Prayer* (1900), pp. vii–xvi; *Encyclopedia Britannica* (1957 ed.), vol. 18, pp. 421–22."[22] After reading the material, there isn't even the slightest inference that government sponsorship of the Book of Common Prayer was at issue. In fact, that book is now the official service manual for the Church of England.

The ancient controversy in England primarily concerned the service of the holy communion, or the Lord's supper, and the use of clerical vestments.[23] It was a struggle between those who wished to retain Roman Catholic practices and the Reformers who wanted "the Protestant purity of worship. The issue was never that of the right of government to sponsor and authorize the Book of Common Prayer."[24]

The basic Puritan view was that the church was not to meddle in the affairs of government. The church and government (or state) were envisioned as serving a ministerial function under God. The government was to be Christian but not administered by the church. The Puritans were not the separationists that Justice Black made them out to be.

The Puritans never questioned governmentally established religion and most assuredly did not leave England and brave the Atlantic Ocean and the American wilderness on that account. Hugo Black's opinion inaccurately interpreted history. His statements, by the testimony of history, must be regarded as not only irrelevant, as the dissenting Justice Stewart averred, but misleading.

Early American Mind

The early Americans in this country held to the belief, commonly accepted in their day, that the establishment of the Christian church by the state governments was both right and necessary. Therefore, it is not surprising that the states had established churches. The idea of the established state church was so firmly settled in their minds that the concept of tolerating all other sects did not exist for the most part.

The idea of a free church in a free state was intended to be no more than a legal separation. In other words, there was no intention by the framers of the Constitution to place church and state each in watertight compartments. From the various activities of the Founding Fathers it is evident that they neither designed nor desired moral and spiritual separation. Separation of government "from ecclesiastical control is not synonymous with separation of religion from" government.[25] If there was any separation at all, it was separation of the church from government but not the Christian faith from government.

We must acknowledge that Christian morality and principles have penetrated all governmental institutions, including the federal government. Total separation of religion and government is a purely theoretical idea which cannot in a free society be enforced except by coercion. History supports the idea that the Christian government that turns to secularism as its mode of operation tends to utilize coercion as a means of separation of church and state. In that instance, the church is devoured by the government.

The Declaration of Independence

The second paragraph of the Declaration of Independence says, "We hold these truths to be self-evident: that all men are created equal; that they are endowed by their Creator with certain unalienable rights; that among these are life, liberty, and the pursuit of happiness." On July 4, 1776, John and Samuel Adams, Benjamin Franklin, Thomas Jefferson and others of like stature expressed their approval of this statement by signing this Declaration.

The Declaration of Independence asserts that God has given man certain rights which no one can take away from him. Particularly mentioned as being of supreme importance are the rights of "life, liberty and the pursuit of happiness."

Justice Black contended that "New York's state prayer program officially establishes the religious beliefs embodied in the Regent's prayer."[26] However, this is also true of the Court's sanctioning of the recitation of the Declaration of Independence and in allowing the public schools to sing "anthems which include the composer's profession of faith in a Supreme Being."[27] There is a contradiction here in Black's reasoning by allowing historical documents which express faith in God to be recited in public schools but forbidding recitation of prayers which express faith in God. The one no more establishes religious beliefs than the other.

If Justice Black's reasoning is carried to its logical conclusion, then the reciting of the Declaration of Independence and its profession of faith are "unconstitutional." The rights of "life, liberty and the pursuit of happiness" embodied in the Declaration are inseparable from faith in the Creator. Therefore, once faith in the Creator is ruled unconstitutional, then the next thing to go is those rights.

Approval and Disapproval

Adverse criticism of the Court's decision was quick in coming. Some of the criticism was emotional and some was politically motivated, but much of it proceeded from sincere and judicious minds. There was a genuine concern that the nation, by the *Engel* decision, was separating itself from its spiritual heritage.

What confused, even shocked, most people was the diversity of opinion voiced by the clergy. Nor could the many contrasting views be separated into the traditional "liberal" and "conservative" positions. There was division in both camps. Bishop James A. Pike and Reinhold Niebuhr, both liberals, attacked *Engel,* but found themselves in opposition to other liberals such as Edwin Dahlberg and Harold E. Fay.[28] Billy Graham deplored the decision as being another step closer to secularization. The liberal magazine *Christian Century* praised the decision, and the conservative *Christianity Today* called it "both defensible and commendable."[29] Unitarians, atheists, agnostics, and most of the Jewish people were overjoyed by the verdict.

The *Washington Post* declared, "It frees schoolchildren from what was in effect a forced participation by rote in an act of worship which ought to be individual, wholly voluntary and devout." Justice Douglas, on the other hand, in his concurring opinion, stated, "There is no element of compulsion or coercion ... a child is free to stand or not stand, to recite or not recite, without fear of reprisal or even comment by the teacher or any other school official."[30] In accord, Justice Tom Clark answered the criticism, saying, "Whether the school prayer was voluntary or not was not decisive." He added that the issue was whether or not the prayer was an establishment of religion.

The liberals rejoiced in the decision because it protected the rights of the individual as against those of the majority. To them, the common good, or general welfare, should be ignored when freedom of individual conscience is at issue. This type of individual "absolutism" has been enhanced by the Court's acceding to the protests of five parents opposing the beliefs and feelings of the majority of the community.[31]

On the whole, public disapproval of the Court's decision far outweighed public approval. The criticism had little effect on the justices. They apparently are no longer limited to and bounded by the words and general spirit of the Constitution. It seems that their biases govern their opinions, and when expressed in the form of case law, they govern other lives as well.

The Aftereffect

Prayer has been largely eliminated from public schools as a result of the *Engel* case. The lower courts overreacted with one court inanely holding that the following prayer recited by kindergarten children was an establishment of religion:

> *We thank you for the flowers so sweet,*
> *We thank you for the food we eat,*
> *We thank you for the birds that sing,*
> *We thank you for everything.*[32]

The Supreme Court, in turn, refused to hear this case on appeal, thereby agreeing with the result.

The short prayer in *Engel* had been instituted as part of a program to foster moral and spiritual training in the schools. With a generation of children who seemed on the verge of running rampant, and with a crisis in the schools, the prayer seemed like a good idea. The Court paid this motive no mind.

Justice William O. Douglas, in his concurring opinion, felt the inscription "In God We Trust" on our coins was an establishment of religion.[33] This inept approach to the First Amendment is a far cry from its true purpose. The Supreme Court, by interfering with the state practice of religion, has in fact violated the First Amendment. More than that, it has uprooted three hundred years of American history.

In the words of Justice Potter Stewart, the only justice to vote against the prayer decision, "The Court has misapplied a great constitutional principle. I cannot see how an 'official religion' is established by letting those who want to say a prayer say it.... I think that to deny the wish of these schoolchildren to join in reciting this prayer is to deny them the opportunity of sharing in the spiritual heritage of our nation."[34] More important, the Court moved a step closer to disestablishing the Christian church.

﹛ 6 ﹜

The Battle for
the Schools
Removing the Light

*I understand there is a practice in Hays [Kansas] of
having Catholic nuns, in uniform, teach in public schools.
And within twenty-four hours after Garth starts school
there I will file a suit challenging that practice.*
                                        Madalyn Murray O'Hair, 1963

When I was seventeen it was a very good year, not only for me
but equally for others. For the schools, however, it turned out to
be another year of dilemma.

For Madalyn Murray O'Hair 1963 proved to be a welcomed
windfall. On the evening of June 17, before a national television
audience, she expressed her satisfaction at the Supreme Court's
two decisions rendered earlier that day invalidating required Bible
reading in the public schools (she had been the plaintiff in one of
the decisions).[1]

She was also extremely gratified to know that she could then
move from Baltimore to Stockton, Kansas, to make preparation to
start an atheist center there. Many looked upon her as a determined civil-liberties advocate while others felt she was an anti-
Christian fanatic. Her later exploits in attempting to spread her
faith of atheism proved the latter to be correct.

The National School Board

Constitutional-law expert Edward S. Corwin was outraged at what he believed were attempts by the United States Supreme Court to set itself up as a national school board. In effect, this is what has happened. The Court has assumed the role of censoring the educational input of the public schools. Specifically, the Court has "confused unconstitutionality with any policy they consider ... socially undesirable."[2] In the tradition of Oliver Wendell Holmes, the Court's personal prejudices are determining the outcome of many cases; the law and its application are no longer primary. In other words, the void left by denying the original meaning of the Constitution has been filled by the subjective determination of judges.

In the process of such judicial semantic juggling the meaning of the Constitution has been twisted—and the schools are without an effective guide to moral and spiritual training. The school officials involved in these cases believed that Scripture reading and prayer were important for this purpose. The Court, however, felt this argument was insignificant.

The fear of some legal jurists is that the Court now thinks of itself as "a priesthood speaking, as in any good theocracy, not of course in their own names but in the name of the silent entity that is incapable of communicating directly with its adherents."[3] The high priests of the Supreme Court, by guiding the conduct of the proletarian priests (the educators) in the furtherance of their faith (the religion of humanity), have eradicated the Christian faith from the public schools.

The War Continues

In the Bible-reading cases the plaintiffs were professed atheists and Unitarians.[4] Atheists believe there is no God. Consequently, the Scriptures tell us, they are fools. There is no such thing as a true atheist. In order for an atheist to be consistent in his belief that there is no God, he would have to be everywhere in the universe at once. This, of course, is impossible for finite man.

The Unitarians, on the other hand, believe there is a God. However, they are not Christians for they repudiate the Christian doctrines of the deity of Christ and the existence of the Trinity.[5] They also regard the Bible as having no more significance than other divine books, such as the "writings of Buddha, Muhammad, Confucius ..." etc.[6]

Our Jewish neighbors, the American Jewish Committee, and the Synagogue Council of America, filed expensive supporting briefs urging that Bible reading be excluded from the public schools. Justice Goldberg, a member of the Court at that time, very likely took notice of the Jewish consternation of this practice.

The aforementioned is not an attempt to belittle the beliefs of others but, simply, an illustration of the spiritual race war manifest in the material world.

Light cannot be darkness, and the scriptural principle cannot be compromised. There are contradiction and conflict here, but no Hegelian "synthesis" can be tolerated without sacrifice of purity of doctrine. What fellowship can light have with darkness?

Mere Belief and Opinions

As has been emphasized, the Supreme Court in 1878 reduced religion to "mere belief and opinions," thereby opening the door to future decisions dealing with religious practices in the public domain. A later Court in 1940 erroneously held that the Fourteenth Amendment had somehow transformed the First Amendment, making it applicable to the states. It followed then that in 1962 the Supreme Court could restrict the religious practice of prayer in the public schools.

It was only a matter of time before the Court would focus on Bible reading in the public schools. The Supreme Court, however, cannot consider an issue until it is sued upon. As usual, there were people waiting to file suit on such a matter.

The Bible-reading Case

Pennsylvania had a state law that *required* that "at least ten verses from the Holy Bible shall be read, without comment, at the opening of each school day."[7] The statute also provided: "Any child shall be excused from such Bible reading, or attending such Bible reading, upon the written request of his parent or guardian."[8] As of 1963, this law had been on the books for fifty years.

In accordance with this statute, each school day at Abington Senior High School opened with a fifteen-minute religious program broadcast over the intercom system as part of a radio and television workshop. A student in the workshop read from the Bible ten verses which were broadcast into every room in the building. This was followed by a recitation of the Lord's Prayer, for which the students were asked to stand in their rooms and to repeat the prayer in unison. In schools having no "intercom" system, the exercise was conducted by a homeroom teacher. She would choose the verses and read them herself or have students read them in rotation or by volunteering. Participation by the students was entirely voluntary. In addition, there were no prefatory statements, no comments or explanations made, and no interpretation was given at or during the exercises.

The parents of two children who were Unitarians sued the school district, alleging violation of the First Amendment religion section, which reads: "Congress shall make no law respecting an establishment of religion, or prohibiting the free exercise thereof."

Madalyn Murray O'Hair's suit involved the very same issues and was, therefore, designated as a companion case. This means it was decided the same day as the *Schempp* case. *Schempp,* being the primary case discussed by the Court, will be one of the two cases treated in this chapter.

The Supreme Court, with Justice Tom Clark writing the *Schempp* opinion, agreed with the parents who brought suit. He held that the establishment clause of the First Amendment, as made applicable to the states via the Fourteenth Amendment, prohibits a state law or a school board from *requiring* that passages from the Bible be read or that the Lord's Prayer be recited in the public schools of a state at the beginning of each school day. This exercise was unconstitutional, Clark stated, even if individual students were excused from attending or participating in such exercises upon written request from their parents. This was an establishment-of-religion case so the freedom-of-religion clause was not an issue here.

Neutralization of the Scriptures

Justice Clark, in the course of the opinion, stated, "We have come to recognize through bitter experience that it is not within the power of government to invade [the] citadel, whether its purpose or effect be to aid or oppose, to advance or retard. In the relationship between man and religion, the state is firmly committed to a position of neutrality.''[9] Clark is saying that in every way government deals with religion it must remain neutral.

As should be clear from the previous chapters, this statement has no basis in history. Many of the men who molded the First Amendment were Christians (and the others based their actions on Christian presuppositions). It is of little surprise then that the First Amendment (as well as the entire Constitution) was written to promote a Christian order.

Moreover, Clark commits the same error as Hugo Black when he confuses the meaning of the terms *religion* and *church*. Reading the Bible doesn't necessarily have anything to do with the church even though it may be deemed religious. The church in this particular situation was definitely not attempting to invade the public schools.

In this decision the Court endeavored to level all religions to a position of equality (with the exception of statist religion) no matter what the tenets of their faith are. In 1833 Justice Story commented on this type of maneuver: "At the time of the adoption of the Constitution ... [an] attempt to level all religions and to make it a matter of state policy to hold all in utter indifference, would have created ... universal indignation" or anger.[10]

The Christian faith is not reducible to the level of every other religion. Christianity offers the only path to the one true God. To hold that the Christian religion is no better than Buddhism or Judaism is blasphemy. To ascribe the same divine authority to the Koran that is possessed by the Christian Scriptures is to deny the very foundation of biblical truth. The Bible is God's Word, not another secular writing.

The Court by seeking to equate Christianity with other religions merely assaults the one faith. The Court is in essence assailing the true God by democratizing the Christian religion. This is suicidal—"All those who hate me love death" (Proverbs 8:36).

Neutrality or Hostility?

While leveling all religions, the Supreme Court did not propose a strict neutrality approach to religion by the government as many seem to believe. The Court takes the position of *accommodation neutrality,* which basically means that whenever the government can favor religion without violating the First Amendment it will do so.

The accommodation-neutrality approach is just as distorted and nonhistorical as other doctrines promulgated by the Supreme Court. The majority of the Court was compelled to take this view simply to stay within the bounds of reason and history.

In answer to the public protest of the prayer case, Justice Clark remarked in 1962, "Most commentators suggested that the Court had outlawed religious observances in the public schools when, in fact, the Court did nothing of the kind." In 1963 he was chosen to write the *Schempp* decision on Bible reading. Seeking to ease the anti-God attacks on the Court, Clark sought to accommodate Christian practices throughout this decision.

The Court recognizes that there is no such animal as absolute or strict neutrality. Likewise, C. Gregg Singer states, "Actually no school system can be neutral in regard to the truths of Scripture for the simple reason that no man can be neutral in regard to the truth of God revealed in Jesus Christ."[11]

Many lower courts and most school administrators are laboring under the illusion that they must be strictly neutral to religion. Such neutrality equals hostility. For example, I can claim to be neutral to the concept of rape. If, however, while looking out my window I notice that a woman is being raped and because of my neutrality I do nothing about it, I am in fact being hostile to that lady. My inaction is hostility.

Therefore, if a school administrator says that he is strictly neutral to religion but that God cannot be mentioned in his school, he is in fact hostile toward religion. And such a man has violated the First Amendment, which provides that the government cannot "prohibit" or forbid religion.

Accommodation Neutrality

Following the accommodation-neutrality approach to religion, the Court has said that not all relationships between government and religion are unconstitutional. There are certain ways in which the state can accommodate religion.

The principle of accommodation-neutrality was best stated by Justice Douglas in the 1952 *Zorach* decision:

> *When the state encourages religious instruction or cooperates with religious authorities by adjusting the schedule of public events to sectarian needs, it follows the best of our traditions. For it then respects the religious nature of our people and accommodates the public service to their spiritual needs.*[12]

As to indifference by the government toward religious groups, which include the public schools, Douglas said:

> *That would be preferring those who believe in no religion over those who do believe. . . . But we find no constitutional requirement which makes it necessary for government to be hostile to religion and to throw its weight against efforts to widen the effective scope of religious influence.*[13]

The *Engel* and *Schempp* cases did not abandon accommodation neutrality but simply defined some of the limits of accommodation.

In the 1970 *Walz* decision the Court reinforced this doctrine by upholding tax exemption for churches. Chief Justice Burger proclaimed, "Short of those expressly proscribed governmental acts there is room for play in the joints productive of a *benevolent neutrality* which will permit religious exercise to exist without sponsorship and without interference."[14]

The Court has clearly designated what "proscribed governmental acts" held in the public schools violate the First Amendment. These are: (1) state-required prayer (*Engel*); (2) state-required Bible reading (*Schempp*); and (3) on-premises religious training (*McCollum*).[15]

Burger specifically noted that adherence "to the policy of neutrality that derives from an accommodation of the establishment and free exercise clauses has prevented the kind of involvement that would tip the balance toward government control of churches or government restraint with religious practice."[16] He was also careful to point out that no "perfect or absolute separation is really possible" and that the First Amendment "seeks to mark boundaries to avoid excessive entanglement'' between church and state.[17]

This decision definitely leaves room for expansion of Christian activities within the public schools. Moreover, in *Schempp* the Court stated that Bible reading is constitutional in literature and history classes within the public schools. As noted in the *Engel* decision, any patriotic hymns or documents that refer to God can be utilized. In fact, religion can be discussed in the public classroom whenever it is relevant to the subject being taught and if it is taught in an objective manner.

The problem that has arisen in the past is that of the lower courts and school administrators who believe strict neutrality is the position of the Court. This is not true. More important, the Burger Court, the present Supreme Court, is not actively hostile to Christianity but will accommodate it when possible.

The concept of accommodation neutrality is vitally important as a presuppositional base for examining religion within the public realm. If a school administrator, or judge for that matter, can be convinced that accommodation neutrality is the Court's approach to religion, then this reduces the possibility that certain Christian religious practices are unconstitutional. If a school administrator, for instance, accepts the fact that the Supreme Court wants to accommodate religion, then he, instead of opposing religion, will seek to *accommodate* it. This principle can aid in bringing Christianity back to public life where it is so desperately needed.

Engel *Extended*

The *Engel* decision held that if the government or the state (the public schools being deemed a part of the state) in any way directs, sponsors, finances, or has an active voice in the Christian religious practice of prayer, then it will be regarded as an establishment of religion prohibited by the First Amendment. The *Schempp* decision, therefore, was merely *Engel* extended to include the prohibition of another Christian religious practice that had been observed in the schools of this country for three hundred years.

Justice Black in *Engel* treated the First Amendment as if it had incorporated by reference certain writings of Jefferson and Madison. This erroneous assumption has become so ingrained in the Court's "thinking" that Justice Clark in *Schempp* made the stark assertion that "the views of Madison and Jefferson, preceded by Roger Williams, came to be incorporated not only in the Federal Constitution but likewise in those of most of our states."[18] History renders this a ridiculous statement.

The Amendment That Never Was

Again, public reaction to the Court's decision was openly hostile. The public resentment was reflected in the activities of Congress. One hundred and forty-six resolutions were introduced into the House of Representatives, each designed to amend the Constitution to overrule the Court's holding.[19]

The most controversial of these resolutions was the proposal offered by Congressman Frank J. Becker of New York. Section one of his proposed constitutional amendment provided: "Nothing in this Constitution shall be deemed to prohibit the offering, reading from, or listening to prayers or biblical scriptures, if participation therein is on a voluntary basis, in any governmental or public school, institution, or place." Section two read: "Nothing in this article shall constitute an establishment of religion."

It is commendable that such an undertaking could originate in a secularized Congress. But criticism of the Becker amendment was forthcoming. The legal periodicals as well as Christian and secular magazines felt this proposal was clearly too reactionary in nature.

In the end an amendment that would have aided in holding onto at least the American tradition was swept away into obscurity. The severance of the spiritual and secular was maintained, and another brick was added to that illusionary wall of separation.

The Obsolete Amendments

It is true, the saying goes, that none is so blind as he who has eyes and will not see. For more than fifty years the Supreme Court has been blind to the realities of the Constitution. The Court has tended to ignore those sections of the document that don't suit its philosophy. Fortunately, the Constitution is intact.

Of special note are the Ninth and Tenth Amendments. The Ninth Amendment reads: "The enumeration in the Constitution of certain rights shall not be construed to deny or disparage others retained by the people." The Tenth says: "The powers not delegated to the United States by the Constitution, nor prohibited by it to the States, are reserved to the States respectively, or to the people."

These two amendments embrace the idea that there are certain rights of so fundamental a character that the federal government may not trespass upon them whether they are enumerated in the Constitution or not. The Tenth Amendment was specifically added to prevent Congress from interfering with the rights of the states or the people, except those granted to Congress in the Constitution.

The fear of an octopean central government occasioned the placing of these amendments into the Constitution. When it now speaks of the Bill of Rights, the Supreme Court audaciously excludes the Ninth and Tenth Amendments, holding that only the first eight amendments compose the Bill of Rights. These amendments are neglected and are called ambiguous by a Court that is usurping the state governmental powers. After all, if the Court can twist and tear the First Amendment as it has done, then why not ignore those sections of the Constitution which limit its power.

Restraining the Tribunal

A cry is echoing throughout the land to crack down on the Supreme Court. Christians and non-Christians alike are demanding that the Court's power be limited.

As a result, several movements have begun in the United States Congress to restrict the Court's jurisdiction. Several congressmen have submitted bills (Senate Bill 283 and House Bill 2414) that would restrain the Supreme Court (as well as lower federal courts) from entering any judgments or decrees denying or restricting voluntary prayer in any public school. These are constitutional measures, because the Constitution, in Article III, Section 2, gives Congress the power to limit the Court's appellate jurisdiction.

It is laudable that such an effort is being made in Congress. Notwithstanding, I believe the crucial issues are being overlooked. First, the reason the Supreme Court is handing down such poor decisions is that for decades non-Christians only have been appointed as justices. And some of the non-Christian justices have worked at being anti-Christian instead of "neutral" to religion. Second, Congress has the initial duty to approve or disapprove all justices appointed by the President to serve on the Court. Consistently, Congress has failed to scrutinize these men or even demand that a Christian be appointed.

There is also a problem with bills or laws designed to limit the Supreme Court's jurisdiction in that the Court over the years has been the lone branch of government one can appeal to with any success in vindicating certain rights. Also, the structure of the federal government is one of delicate balance, and one branch should invade another's territory only in extreme emergencies.

The point is this: it is a dangerous step for Congress to limit the Court's jurisdiction. If, more appropriately, Congress performed its duties satisfactorily in the first place, there would be much less of a problem with the Court than now.

Finishing off God

The Society of Separationists was founded by Madalyn Murray O'Hair in 1963. It boasts a membership of 60,000 hard-core atheists in the country.

One of the more active chapters is located in Richmond, Virginia. The group's main goals are focused on the eradication of "In God We Trust" as a national motto, the cancellation of postage stamps which say "Pray for Peace," and the abolition of tax exemptions for church property.

The current head of the group, B. Meredith Winn, Jr., sums up their objectives:

> *The group wants to remove the words "under God" from the Pledge of Allegiance and to challenge legislative prayers at all levels of government, religious services in the White House, prayers at athletic games and commencements in tax-supported schools, distribution of Gideon Bibles in schools, and Easter and Christmas holidays from schools.... Also, it wants to challenge the swearing in of public officials, court witnesses, Civil Serv-*

ice employees, armed forces personnel, jury members, and others in government situations by "so help me God" and the setting aside of days of prayer by presidents and governors ... separationists want to stop government money from going to religious schools and hospitals in any way, whether by scholarship, grants or building aid. Also, the group wants to challenge Internal Revenue Service tax exemptions connected with religion, such as church contributions, and United Fund–Community Chest financing of religious-connected organizations.[20]

The Scriptures refer to the atheist as a fool because he says, "There is no God" (Psalm 14:1). A fool is commonly defined as a person lacking in understanding. In addition, the Scriptures indicate that he who does not respect and know God has neither wisdom nor understanding (Proverbs 9:10). Men tend to flee what they do not understand. They create the illusion that God is not. But their pretending does them no good. God is, and in the end He will judge them.

The Society of Separationists has been successful in its drives against prayer and Bible reading in the public schools. The members have organized and accumulated power. Christians must do the same in order to fulfill the scriptural mandate to be the "salt" or preservative of society. The public schools are a good place to build the foundation for cultural change. The atheists have proven this.

The Religion of Secularism

The renowned educator Horace Mann fought to establish statist education by erecting the public schools. He campaigned equally hard against sectarianism, but he earnestly contended for Bible reading in public schools. Writing in *Education and Liberty* in 1952, James B. Conant, after noting Mann's stance on Bible reading in the public schools, commented:

One hopes that the events of the next fifty years will not prove that he was wrong. The charge that the public schools, being nonsectarian, are "godless" is at least a century old. What is new in recent years is the religious

*dogmatism of certain groups which has made impossible
even the reading of the Bible without comment in the public schools of some states and localities.*[21]

Conant's fear was well placed. More important, however, was
the anti-Christian tone then beginning to pervade the Supreme
Court. An effective move had been made by the federal government to restrict religious exercises within the realm of its recognized church, the public schools. If the children were not taught
Christianity, then they very likely would not know it. How then
could this become a Christian nation?

Justice Potter Stewart, the only dissenter in the *Schempp* decision, recognized rather astutely what had taken place: "A refusal
to permit religious exercises . . . is seen, not as the realization of
state neutrality, but rather as the establishment of a religion of secularism, or at the least, as government support of the beliefs of
those who think that religious exercises should be conducted only
in private."[22] The religion of secularism, as Justice Stewart says,
is the established religion of this country.

A Nation Without a Constitution

At his inaugural ceremony, the President of the United States
is given the oath of office; with right hand on the holy Bible, the
President avows, "I solemnly swear to support and defend the
Constitution of the United States." What is tragic is that many
Presidents have made a solemn oath on the Word of the sovereign
God they know nothing about.

Those who strive to isolate religion completely from government, business, and education are in reality attempting to destroy
the Christian religion. While trying to make this country free from
religion, they are destroying the nation. There is no reason the
government and the Christian religion cannot cooperate and work
together. This is the American tradition that was intended to be
protected by the First Amendment.

The United States Supreme Court should be restricted to following the intent of those who drafted the First Amendment. To
pretend that we are still governed by a document that is little
adhered to is illusion. If the Court can flout the intention of our

governing document, then we are no longer under a constitutional government. *If* it can be successfully argued that the conditions and climate of the modern day are so very different from those in which the framers of the Constitution lived, then, like the Founding Fathers, the Constitution may have outlived its time.

When he was a representative from Arizona, John B. Conlan summed it up well:

> *The Constitution is no better than the five out of nine men that you have on the Supreme Court at any point in time. What the constitutional fathers meant when they created that document and that contract among the people, is one thing. It may not mean the same to someone else two hundred years later, even though it should. But depending on whom you have in the presidency and whom you have in the Senate, who confirms or rejects presidential appointment, will determine what your Constitution means, if anything at all. The fact that we have a great Constitution, in itself, means nothing.*[23]

₹ 7 ₹

Valley of the Bones

The whole world is in my hand, and I will conquer and subjugate the world.

Sun Myung Moon

To taste the sea all one needs is one gulp.

Aleksandr I. Solzhenitsyn

When I was in high school in 1962 and 1963, it was of little importance to me that the highest court in the land had "outlawed" prayer and Bible reading in public schools. This was not the specific holding in these cases, according to the Court, but the secularized public schools interpreted the decisions to mean just that.

The point is that Christ or God was of no issue in my high school, anyway. God had been relegated to brief and inconsequential mention. The technological society with its computerized world view had already conquered the system. The statist ceiling had been drawn over the children's heads. The easiest way to prevent children from poking holes in the secular umbrella and reaching out to God was to eradicate mention of Him. "Let's pretend He doesn't exist and He will go away," they reasoned.

Suddenly, however, something had gone awry. Where life once flourished in the public schools, death now prevails. Where peace was once the rule, rebellion is now the practice. A past duped generation of teachers is now teaching a presently duped generation of students. And the panic button has been pushed.

In 1975 there were over 75,000 reported assaults by students on public-school teachers. The figure ignores the fact that many teachers fail to report attacks on their person and property from fear of student reprisal or of intimidation by school officials (such attacks look bad on reports to supervisors).

Until some seventy years ago the Christian religion controlled the schools in this country. The schools, however, eventually fell to public education. The state or government now rules godlike over public schools. The Christian God, as a result, has gradually but effectively been removed from the schools. The flesh has been slowly rotting on the state body. The skeleton has emerged, and we now find ourselves viewing things from the Valley of the Bones.

The Hitler Youth

Adolf Hitler understood the importance of the youth of his country. In 1922 he proclaimed, "Upon their shoulders rests the future of our Fatherland."[1] Hitler thereupon set out to determine the education of the children of Germany.

Employing the Lockean theory that the mind at birth is a clean slate, Hitler sought to form the ultimate man. To accomplish this, however, the education system would have to be administered by the government. The state could then mold the child into whatever it desired.

Startlingly, the children and young people of Germany voluntarily joined the crazed Hitler youth movement. No coercion was necessary. In 1932 there were fewer than one million members of Hitler's youth, but by 1939 the movement had swollen to eight million.

To understand this phenomenon, the pre-Hitler youth must be studied. Astonishingly enough, valid parallels can be drawn comparing the modern American youth (as well as that of most countries of the world) with the pre-Hitler youth of Germany.

The German youth of the late 1920s and early 30s had become alienated from the older generation. They were questioning the old order. Marxism and pure democratic thought had permeated a country that had recently suffered humiliating defeat in World War I. The traditional authorities of the school, the church, and the family were now suspect. The children sought escape from the bleak world of the "establishment." As one particular avenue of escape from an environment they believed oppressive, "They left home at weekends and during school or university holidays with tent, rucksack, and guitar, hiking through Germany north to south, east to west, discovering for themselves the quiet beauty of the German countryside ... in search of something new. They turned to an age gone by, epitomized by the romantic element in most of Wagner's operas, and around the campfires they sat singing the ballads of old. Folklore experienced a renaissance."[2]

The analogy to today's American youth is quite appropriate. The modern young person is seeking escape. The church is a dry well, offering the children very little in the way of fulfillment. The public school is worse.

The youth of Germany, though divided, began to unite in small organizations. Diversified, they had no power. To have unity they needed a common deliverer.

The young people of Germany were wandering and searching. Then Hitler walked onto the scene. The decadent society was not ready for him, but the hungering youth now had their messiah. He recognized them publicly, and by drawing on the common factors of rejection of the old and pursuit of the new, Hitler sucked the very power and strength of the youth from the established order. He was energy, he was change, and he united them. They sought re-creation in his image.

Individualism came to be despised. It was the enemy of unity, the antithesis of statist collectivism.

Likewise, the authority of the old could not stand over the young. The Hitler youth began to assault the schoolteachers both physically and verbally. To stop the open attack on school authorities, Hitler himself had to step in and restrain his youth. His government eventually had to move in and bring the school within the dominion of the fuehrer.

Christian education was increasingly restricted until it was eliminated. Hitler established his own schools. Paramilitary training became the primary function of the school. The traditional aims of education—reading, writing, arithmetic—became secondary.

Children were taken from their families because they were now part of the nation.[3] They no longer belonged to their parents. They were the property of the government.

The shibboleth was, "You are nothing, your people is everything." Unity was to be found no longer in God but in man. No more were they to serve God; they were to serve mankind through their messiah.

The German church, although protesting such acts of Hitler as his legalization of euthanasia, on the whole compromised. They too saw hope in the new leader. His open avowals that the Jews must be purged seemed to slip by unnoticed. By the time his true aims became apparent, he was the god of the system. It was too late to protest or call for change.

The American youth are wandering. They feel they have no home. The family structure has been so weakened that it is of little importance to the "turned-on" youth. Authority over them is a matter of oppression. As one young high school student body president remarked before his school board, "We are tired of being told what to do. Old people have been dictating to us too long." This is the general feeling among American youth. The question is: Where is it leading?

The Pied Piper

The basic shortcoming of the new left of the late sixties and early seventies in the United States was that they never came together in a united front. The revolutionary zeal and will to destroy were there, but a unified purpose was lacking. The youth movement was looking to mystics like Bob Dylan and the Beatles for unity.[4] It simply wasn't to be found in music and drugs.

The search for unity still exists. A meeting of "America's radical movement" held in Texas in 1975 was an attempt to bring together the leftist youth. Despair was the obvious outcome as hopes for a unifier lingered on. Robb Burlage, who helped Tom Hayden form the Students for a Democratic Society, lamented the disunity of the American left, "We've been so purged ... we've lost any sense of how to reintegrate."[5]

As was the case of the pre-Hitler youth, the post-American youth of today are looking into the past to escape the dismal order of the establishment. The current craze is focused on the fifties, when the young were "cool."

The youth groups are still around; they've just gone underground. In the large cities youth gangs are growing. The seed is there, awaiting the energizing force that will activate germination.

It is the Christian's task to provide leadership for the youth. If the Christian will not fill this void, then a stable government is needed to provide leadership. Neither is present. The probabilities of the mysterious uniting leader being out there somewhere at this moment in time are high. There are many voices calling the young to them. One isolated instance, if it is merely isolated, is that of the Reverend Sun Myung Moon, whose followers vehemently assert he is the Lord of the second advent, the third Adam, the new messiah. The fervor of his disciples has caused alarm in both Christian and non-Christian circles.

With a supposed membership of "2,000,000 active and associate members in 120 countries, Moon states that he will conquer the world."[6] With devoted attention to his commands, his disciples have found that unity and purpose needed by the modern youth. He tells them, "I am the thinker. I am your brain."[7] Forget individualism and "come together" in unity in the Reverend Mr. Moon.

Moon doesn't seek to eradicate the Jew from society, as Hitler did, but believes it is the pervasive Communist forces that are threatening. He says, "The present United Nations must be annihilated by our power. That is the stage for the Communists."[8] Hitler had his scapegoat, and so does the Reverend Mr. Moon.

The authority of family and country is also lost to this new messiah. He commands his followers to deny "past families, friends, neighbors, and relatives."[9] Further, "I want to have the members under me who will be willing to obey me even though they may have to disobey their own parents and the Presidents of their own nations. And if I gain half the population of the world, I can turn the whole world upside down."[10]

A New York rabbi, Maurice Davis, believes Moon is serious and frightening. Rabbi Davis is the leader of a group called Citizens Engaged in Reuniting Families. In February 1975 he told an informal congressional hearing in Washington, D.C., "The last time I witnessed a movement that had these characteristics—a single authoritarian head, fanatical followers, absolute unlimited funds, hatred for everyone on the outside, suspicion against their parents—was the Nazi youth movement. And I tell you, I'm scared."[11]

Christ, in Matthew 24:5, warned of false messiahs seeking to deceive. To a generation without the Scriptures, this means very little. Yet the time is nearly ripe for a youth fuehrer. The one missing link is the type of severe economic depression that brought men like Hitler and Mussolini to power. And that may not be far off. That plus the ability to play the right tune and the youth fuehrer, like the pied piper, may be able to bring forth a huge monolithic and unified following. The pied piper I read about, though, led all the rats into the river to drown.

The Child as Property

Hitler envisioned children as the property of the government. Moon foresees the child as the possession of his new government. Individuality, such reasoning holds, must recede before a mystical communal education. In this type of system, the child becomes merely another extension of the totalitarian state.

The prime responsibility for the education of the child in a "free" society belongs to the parent. The Supreme Court, by way of its decisions concerning the Christian religion, has challenged this parental responsibility. With its decisions, the Court has assumed the right to become the national school board, thereby determining the curriculum of the school.[12] Like a grand inquisitor, the Court has taken upon itself to decide what the child will or will not be taught.

It has always been a source of pride in the United States that the children are not the charge of the state but are under the direct control of the parents. Children, according to the Scriptures, do not belong to Caesar, as is the case in Russia and other totalitarian countries. The Supreme Court decisions pose a serious problem in this respect. The prime responsibility for educating the child has shifted to the government. The anxiety of the Christian parent is heightened as he watches the state removing nearly every reference to the Christian heritage from education.

The Scriptures clearly make the education of a child the responsibility of the parents within the sphere of the family. Proverbs 22:6 states, "Train up a child in the way he should go, even when he is old he will not depart from it." This charge, coming from God to parents, gives them certain rights and responsibilities above and beyond the government (or state). Parents are the true architects of their children's destinies, and an extremely important element of this foundation is education.[13]

The issue finally boils down to whether the child is an individual under the authority and guidance of the family, or whether he is considered a government parcel of property, measurable in dollars and cents. That the child is a person created in the image of God gives him tremendous worth. On the other hand, if the child is considered a highly developed animal by way of evolutionary chance, then he is a thing. Things, however, tend to depreciate according to the statist market value.

The Schizoid Child

The exclusion of religion from the public schools has the effect of impressing a schizoid personality upon the child who is reared in the Christian home.[14] The schizophrenic is torn in two by split personalities. Likewise, the Christian child is torn by two cultures. He is forced to compartmentalize his life: one *large* area has no reference to God, and one *very limited* area is given the privilege of religious activity.[15]

The basic world for the modern child is the school. If the school is godless, then it is logical to assume that most who attend will be godless.

The schizophrenic division of the child's life in his early school days will very likely effect a similar separation in his later business and social life. This splitting of culture will express itself in alienation of the child not only from God and other human beings but from himself as well.

The child's spirit is a single unit. It cannot be severed into two parts. The spirit is very active and needs to express itself. To exclude prayer from the child's curriculum has the effect of placing on the soul a straitjacket which is difficult for the parent to remove. Likewise, "to be forced to use the materials of this creation while denying their Creator is bound to have a baneful effect."[16]

The secularization of the public school has compelled the child to assume the task of learning a fragmented culture. For three hundred years Bible reading and prayer have been part of the American culture. Surely, the public schools were only fulfilling their task in recognizing this American heritage, thereby transmitting the *total* culture.[17] If the public schools fail at their basic task, then we can only expect a fragmented man.

The Functionless Family

The family emerges from the Scriptures as the basic unit within society. The family is where man first learns religion and self-government as well as his total education.

The Christian religion is a product of the family. In order to destroy the Christian religion, the family must be anesthetized.

Self-government in the same way is a function of the family. To rid a man of the conscious need of self-government, the family must be decimated.

The family was instituted by God to be a form of government in a chaotic world populated by fallen men. Destroy the family and anarchy results, and as history teaches us, anarchy leads to totalitarianism. Chaos needs not only control, but coercive control to keep down the rebellion of anarchy.

Capture the child and loosen him from the confines of the family and the family is reduced to an institution without function. The Supreme Court has moved in this direction, and now a scandalized Congress is also edging toward that course.

The Mondale-Brademas Child and Family Services Act of 1975 (S. 626, H.R. 2966), which arbitrarily declares that the government is a partner to parents, is a piece of legislation which demands some scrutiny. President Nixon vetoed the bill in 1971, stating, "To adopt the bill would commit the vast authority of the national government to the side of communal approaches to child rearing."

The 1975 version of the bill creates a new federal agency—the Office of Child and Family Services—which is to be part of the already gargantuan Department of Health, Education, and Welfare.

The bill advocates day-care centers, but its basic intent is to set up a comprehensive child-development program. When a parent requests the aid of this new agency, the authority of the agency is extended even over the private home. For example, agents are sent into the home to take charge of the child in the parents' place.

The bill basically declares that as a matter of *children's rights* the government must exert control over the family. The child must be placed into the care of the state, not the parents. It recognizes that communal forms of upbringing have an "unquestionable" superiority over all other forms.

A clue as to what may be "acceptable" child rearing to the Washington government may be found in *MACOS (Man: A Course of Study)*, a federally developed social-science program in which ten-year-old children are taught to view wife-swapping, infanticide, cannibalism, and euthanasia as just different ways of doing things, or as merely cultural differences.[18]

Parental rights conflict with the child's rights under this legislation. Parents can be reported to the federal agency by their own children for stepping beyond the bounds of federal regulation.

Parental rights are further diluted by the definition of the term *parent* in the bill. *Parent* is defined as "any person who has primary day-to-day responsibility for *any* child." Therefore, the day-care center workers who supervise the child on a day-to-day basis become "parents." The natural parents are made to give up even their role title.

There is also a bill before Congress, the Youth Safety Act (Senate bill 422), which gives the federal government direct power and control over private camps, their directors, and the children who attend camps. Again, parental control over children in the camps is greatly curtailed. If this bill passes, then children could be required to attend camps in the same manner as the Hitler youth were.

The only function that seems to be left to the family is procreation of offspring. This too is threatened by modern science and its progress in the area of "in-vitro" development of the fetus; or, as it is better known, test-tube babies. This is not a future-oriented statement, for fetuses are being grown in the laboratory today.[19]

It is evident that if this stream of insanity is not "turned back" soon, this country faces a demoralizing and devastating future. The way back home is clear. The nation must look to God instead of to man for answers. Christians must rear their children in the way of the Lord. The place to begin is in the family, and it must continue into the classroom.

The Unique Problem

The public schools and the practices of the Christian religion therein have drawn special interest by many, including the Supreme Court. As the highest legal order of the secular government, the Supreme Court has become the inquisitor for the system. Why has the Court been so intent on removing the Christian religion from the public schools?

Justice Brennan, in his concurring opinion in the 1963 *Schempp* decision, pointed out that "religious exercises in the public schools present a unique problem."[20] The uniqueness of the problem originates from the fact that in this particular instance children are the main concern.

The Supreme Court has intimated more than once in its decisions that "intimidation" by religion is to be avoided. Children, the Court holds, are young and very easily influenced. They are a captive audience in the sense that they are compelled to attend school. In other words, the children are not present of their own free will.

Amid all the concern over Christian religious practices in public schools the cry often heard is, "What happens if God is removed from the school grounds?" Justice Goldberg in *Schempp*, taking the position of accommodation neutrality, aptly pointed out that hostility toward the Christian religion would develop if viewed from a position of strict neutrality:

> *Untutored devotion to the concept of neutrality could lead to ... results which partake not simply of that noninterference and noninvolvement with the religious which the Constitution commands, but of a broadening and pervasive devotion to the secular and a passive, or even active, hostility to the religious. Such results are not only not compelled by the Constitution, but, it seems to me, are prohibited by it.*[21]

Justice Tom C. Clark, who wrote the opinion in *Schempp*, affirmatively said that "the state may not establish a 'religion of secularism' in the sense of affirmatively opposing or showing hostility to religion, thus 'preferring those who believe in no religion over those who do believe.' "[22]

The Court definitely senses the danger of their own decisions concerning prayer and Bible reading. Weak affirmations such as those above, however, have a habit of being overlooked and ignored.

Basically, the children have now become a captive audience to the "religion of secularism." It is the content of what is taught to the children in such a situation that causes alarm. The modern child is taught that he developed by chance from an animal. For example, recently a teacher in Los Angeles was overheard instructing her kindergarten class to pray to their teddy bears. From teddy bears it is but one short step to the worshipping of metal idols.

The Violent Generation

Violence is running rampant in the public schools. There is no God above these children, the state believes, who is judging their actions and holding them accountable. All that exists above them is the protective umbrella of the statist god. In 1965 there were no security guards in the public schools of Chicago. Today there are over 700.

In 1975 over $10 million was spent on combating crime, violence, and vandalism in the public schools of the United States.[23] Investigating the scope of crime in the public schools of this country, a Senate committee found that "between 1970 and 1973 school-related homicides increased by eighteen percent, rapes and attempted rapes increased by forty percent, robberies went up thirty-seven percent, assaults on students soared eighty-five percent, and assaults on teachers jumped seventy-seven percent."[24]

Student violence directed toward property in the public schools has prompted the school systems to petition Congress for $300 million to aid in making up the loss.[25] Total property loss for 1975 will top $600 million as a result of vandalism, burglary, arson, thefts, and student extortion.[26]

After hearing testimony by students and educators in 1975 concerning "gangs shooting up classrooms, teacher assaults, and extortions carried on by fourth graders," Congress asked the Justice Department's Law Enforcement Assistance Administration to help wipe out such crimes.[27]

The situation in the schools is so out of hand that at Crenshaw High School in Los Angeles teachers are wearing wrist transmitters. If violence erupts, the teacher pushes the alarm button on her wrist transmitter, which alerts the central station. A school guard with a walkie-talkie is notified and hurries to assist the teacher.[28]

In Washington, D.C., police sergeant Thor Bevens pointedly remarked, "I could set up police substations in a couple of these schools and there would be enough crime for a squad of men to make arrests steadily through the day." He reported that most of the teachers assaulted daily in the schools make no reports. He has instead found that "many more teachers retire on disability than policemen and firemen. What you need in Washington are combat teachers."[29]

Violent student aggression is aimed not only at teachers but at fellow students as well. A survey conducted in Dade and Broward counties in Florida showed that twenty-five percent of the students there feared bodily harm while in the schools.[30]

The great monolith of secularism is leading to anarchy. The schools, at the cost of striving to keep peace, have sacrificed a generation to semiliteracy. *Newsweek's* excellent analysis of this problem in its article "Why Johnny Can't Write" has shown that young people graduating from high schools can't read or write effectively.[31] The public schools are producing a generation of irresponsible people. Irresponsible people must be led because they can't lead. *In God's place*

Church historian Reverend Martin E. Marty, associate dean of a University of Chicago divinity school and an associate editor of *Christian Century* magazine, predicts that in the near future people will become tired of the "delicacy of freedom."[32] They will be looking for a leader to impose what he calls "a gentle Maoism," an order they can trust more than their own ability to choose.[33]

By removing the Christian religion from the public schools, secular educators and the Supreme Court have taken away the only objective standard by which people can effectively operate. If I believe there is no God to judge me, and if my teachers tell me that when I destroy, society is to blame, then I am driven by impulse, not by God's standards. What is worse is the fact that this mode of thinking leads to despair. In despair people reach out and grab security. Without God, the security of the modern man is in the state or the government. That is no security at all.

The Skeleton

The word *religion* is nowhere defined in the Constitution. This means that to define religion one must seek elsewhere.

The Supreme Court has by no means explicitly defined what religion means in the Constitution. The Court, however, held that the prayer in the *Engel* decision was an establishment of a religion.

It is obvious that the meaning of religion goes far beyond the belief in God. It covers religions that do not believe in the existence of God. The term can even include a "religion of secularism." *Ante Christ*

The highly respected Justice Felix Frankfurter in 1961 gave a broad definition of religion: "By its nature, religion—in the comprehensive sense in which the Constitution uses that word—is an aspect of human thought and action which profoundly relates the life of man to the world in which he lives."[34] Applying such a broad definition to the public schools would essentially mean that the teaching of any subject matter that "profoundly relates the life of man to the world in which he lives" would be to teach religion. If a certain material is taught objectively and is relative to the subject matter of the secular course, it would seem permissible even if it is the teaching of religion (according to the Court). The difficulty arises, however, in the teaching of moral values and principles which are intended to influence the lives of students.

The Court indirectly alludes to this particular problem in the *Schempp* decision by recognizing the possibilities of the government establishing a "religion of secularism" in the public schools. This occurs when the state affirmatively opposes or exhibits hostility to religion by "preferring those who believe in no religion to those who believe."

The schools have argued in the religion cases that by taking God out of the schools a void is left which is quickly filled by the "religion of secularism," or more correctly, the religion of humanity. This argument was regarded as invalid by the Court because neutrality is the position to be favored toward religion in the public schools.

But what of the public school that is supposedly neutral toward the narrower definition of religion but that teaches moral values and principles? In a national survey of school principals and school district administrators taken in the late 1960s as part of a congressional hearing on prayer, 99.4 percent replied yes in response to the following question: "Do the aims and objectives of your school system include the teaching of moral values?" (Moral values refer to such qualities as honesty, courage, loyalty, etc.) And 78.71 percent replied yes to a second question: "Do the aims and objectives of your school system include the teaching of spiritual values?'' (Spiritual values refer to such qualities as love, faith, reverence for a Supreme Being, etc.)[35]

Such teaching is definitely aimed at influencing and forming the lives of schoolchildren. It "is an aspect of human thought and action which profoundly relates the life of man to the world in which he lives." It is not an objective academic course taught for the purpose of disseminating knowledge. Moral values and principles have always been concerned with whether an act is right or wrong, good or bad, and what a person should be. Historically, these have been religious concerns. *deception* ↗

The argument to come in the future is that the teaching of moral values and principles in the allegedly neutral school in effect establishes a school religion which is centered around nontheistic principles. This is *affirmative* action by the local board. Certainly then the teaching of moral values is fraught with the same evils that the Supreme Court believes the First Amendment was intended to prohibit.

Children in public schools who embrace moral values different from those taught in the schools are made to feel inferior and isolated. "A child could be led to believe that nontheistic values are more important than theistic values, because the influence of the public school is behind them."[36]

It is apparent, therefore, that the teaching of moral values and principles in a local school can have the effect of a religion and that such a practice is religious. One lower federal court indicated awareness of this problem: "It seems clear that, in light of the decided cases, the public schools as between theistic and humanistic religions, must carefully avoid any program of indoctrination in ultimate values."[37] *The Devil is cunning. Oh how I love Jesus*

The logical conclusion of the results of the Supreme Court decisions regarding Christian religious practices is the establishment of a public-school system which teaches mere technicalities and nothing else. The teacher may state or inform the students that the murder of millions of Jews by Hitler is a historical fact. As to whether it is right or wrong, or good or bad, the teacher will be instructed to remain silent for fear of self-incrimination. The schools then become a skeleton of mathematics and facts, nothing more, nothing less. The eventual result of the ungod society is the uneducated, spiritually dead man. The schools are already in the process of being reduced to a therapeutic adjustment center geared to produce a social animal.

Paul Simon put it well in his song *Kodachrome:*

When I think back on all the crap I learned in high school
It's a wonder I can think at all
And though my lack of education hasn't hurt me none
I can read the writing on the wall.
Kodachrome, they give us those nice bright colors
They give us the greens of summer
Makes you think all the world's a sunny day....[38]

The cold, hard world is not a sunny day. The secular school may present it that way, but the one who believes it is a victim of illusion.

The Curse

The Scriptures firmly promise that those who turn away from God to idols will be cursed until at least "the third and fourth generations" (Exodus 20:5). To those who "go astray in their heart" not knowing Him, God states that "they shall not enter My rest" (Psalm 95:10, 11; Hebrews 3:10, 11).

I believe this present generation is under such a curse. They have literally become "the children of the damned." They are men without the Bible and, therefore, without knowledge. They worship a phenomenon called man. Instead of acknowledging the Creator, they trust in the theory of evolution. No longer do men claim to be made in the image of God; by chance they have developed into the image of the beast.

In the eyes of God men have tremendous value. They are of such value that He gave His life for all men. In the eyes of godless men, however, other men have very little value. They are, in fact, disposable. God has given depraved men over to their lusts. Modern men have no guidance except that of other fallen creatures. A people that will not be governed by God will be governed by fallen man. Men of nations that have rejected God are left to the whimsical insanity of godless men.

In H. W. Koch's book, *Hitler Youth: The Duped Generation,* a young Hitlerite taken prisoner at the end of the war tells the story of his incarceration at the liberated concentration camp Dachau. Upon entering the camp with several other young German prisoners, under the guidance of American servicemen, they began work. After prying open the doors of a freight truck inside the Dachau camp, the young Hitlerite describes the horror of the event, "The first thing that fell out was the skeleton of a woman. After that nothing more fell out, for dead bodies were standing so close to each other, like sardines, that one supported the other ... the next thing we were taken to was a red brick building enveloped by an acrid smell. We entered a hall and, for a moment, we thought we were in a big boiler room with a number of big stoves. That idea was immediately dispelled when we saw before each stove a stretcher made of metal with iron clamps. Some of these stretchers were still halfway in the stove covered by the remnants of burnt bodies. That night was a sleepless one. The impact of what we had seen was too great to be immediately digested. I could not help but cry."[39]

≀ 8 ≀

The Beginning of the End

Disestablishment

The state will not tolerate any gods besides itself.
                                        Erik von Kuehnelt-Leddihn

They only consult to cast him down from his excellency:
they delight in lies: they bless with their mouth, but
they curse inwardly.
                                        Psalm 62:4 (KJV)

When in 1962 Hugo Black issued his opinion in the *Engel* deci-sion, which banned state-directed prayer from public schools, shock waves rolled across the nation. Although the public outcry against the Court's decision was great, it was met by many as a mixed blessing of vindication and liberty. Over three hundred years of American tradition were uprooted and cast to the winds. Amid the jumbled choruses of joy and consternation many people were asking, "What is happening to this country when our children can't recite a simple prayer to begin the school day?" The door to the God of the Bible seemingly had been closed. Suddenly there was an emptiness in the schoolhouse. It was, however, only a reflection of the emptiness in the country.

The Eden Syndrome

Modern man, taken as a whole, has fallen prey to the same temptation Eve fell for in the garden. That is, she desired to be as God, possessing the capacity to determine for herself what is good and what is evil (Genesis 3:5).

God, however, has imposed His absolutes upon the universe, thus denying man's capacity to decide certain issues. Everything operates on this basis. The law of gravity, for instance, says that when I drop an egg from my apartment window two stories above the ground, it will descend rather than ascend. And if someone or something doesn't intervene to arrest its descending flight, then it will splatter on impact.

Mathematics operates on the same principle. Two plus two always equals four. This fact disturbs the existential mentality, but it nevertheless consistently holds true.

There are countless examples of the cause-and-effect mechanism that propels our existence to its eventual culmination. It is this very absolutism of God, however, that humanistic men seek to stave off, especially in the area of moral absolutes. It cannot be circumvented in reality; therefore, it is circumvented in unreality. The illusion and the lie surface.

First of all, humanistic man, in the same spirit of Satan's query, questions God's absolutes: "Indeed has God said ..." (Genesis 3:1). The temptation "you will be like God" (Genesis 3:5) lures man to assume that he is just as capable as God in deciding what is good and bad. For a while he is a partner of God, but the more man questions, the more he feels that he can separate himself from God's absolutes. Man then declares, "I am separate and autonomous!" Finally, man decides that no longer is he created in the image of God, but is, instead, created in the image of man.

Darwin, however, threw a monkey wrench into the wheel. Instead of God's creating man or man's creating man, a god called chance developed man. Man is now formed in the image of beasts. He begins looking to the amoeba for answers instead of to God. The amoeba, however, can't tell the humanist what he needs to know. Darwinism asserted that people were simply blobs of cells moving aimlessly through space. Purpose and meaning are lost. Man is no longer a creature of value imaging the living God. He is a disposable animal.

The humanist's belief that he has separated himself from God has cost him any concept of reality. He screams, "There are no truths. I know nothing but myself (whatever that is)." This is despair, and the classic way around despair is to lie—create the illusion. It's the philosophy of "I'll tell you a lie if you'll tell me a lie." This kind of thinking leaves room for someone like Black Muslim Muhammad Ali to conclude, "Man desires to understand that which he cannot understand. You give the people a shark named Jaws. They like that. They want to understand that. Give 'em the plain simple truth and they don't believe it. People love to be lied to."[1]

Why all the lies? Well, if a man comes to realize that absolutes exist and that there is rationality and order to the universe, then he is confronted with the Author of order and objectivity, the Creator. Instead of recognizing truth he recedes into the void of fantasy.

Humanistic man proclaims throughout the earth, "Rejoice! God is dead!" The problem here, however, is the fact that if God is dead, man is also dead. He is simply another worthless cog in an irrational existence. Man begins to view man as a machine. Modern men have no value. They are disposable.

Stalin said that in order to create his omelet he would have to break some eggs. As a result of this type of reasoning, countless millions of people were murdered in the Soviet Union. The lies and illusions carried to their logical conclusions lead to despair, and destruction.

god

Modern man fallaciously believes he is a god. To perpetuate his godliness, however, he requires the state (or government) to manifest his god function. The government, in effect, represents humanistic man in his quest to be God.

Notwithstanding, history demonstrates that the state eventually turns on its former master, biting the very hand that feeds it. In fact, to paraphrase Augustine: "The state that abandons God is no better than a band of robbers." The government becomes power-hungry and begins to eat its inhabitants. It literally swallows the individuality of man, and man now becomes "the masses." His value on the stock market of the state is extremely low.

They refuse God and His truth

Manipulation develops in relation to the masses. If, as neo-Darwinian thought has it, man is moving in a deterministic environment that simply exists in time, then why not manipulate that environment to produce a better product? The government intervenes in the planning, seeking to predestinate man's fate. "If man is not good then let's make him good" is the philosophy of the state.

Supposing God dead, the government steps in to fill the vacuum left by His absence. But once the state assumes the god-function, man has no appeal beyond the government. When this god speaks with final authority, man is lost. The Christian can burst through the umbrella that the state places over man and communicate with the God of the Scriptures. The non-Christian, however, is left with the cold mechanism of governmental politics over which he has no control. After all, a god would not be a god if it could be controlled.

The God Conspiracy

The center of attention in any given legal system is the lawgiver. The great biblical lawgiver, the prophet Moses, was the central attraction of his particular era. Moses, however, was simply a lawgiver and just that. He recognized that the true God existed above and beyond him. More important, the legislature or the source of law was that God. Moses simply served to pass on God's law to His people. He knew that there "is only one lawgiver and judge, the one who is able to save and destroy" (James 4:12).

Law, in the Christian sense, begins and ends with the God of the Scriptures. His commands and communication issue forth in the form of His Word. This propositional truth is recorded in the Bible.

Where law is promulgated (or made), and where law is limited or terminated, is the highest point in any particular governmental system. The highest point in any system, society, or state is the authority or god of that state, whether it be a king, a legislature, or a court.

Through the process of rejecting the transcendent Christian God, humanistic man has in turn looked down to nature and the beasts. In most ways man then becomes as irresponsible as the beasts. Obviously, the irresponsible cannot govern. They have to be fed. This results in something like the welfare system.

Modern man, though deifying himself, manifests this deity through the state which then assumes the god-function. But it is the lawgiver or legislator who is the source of law which prevails in the humanistic order. Whatever reaches ascendancy in the system is the god of that system.

We the people of the United States find that the Supreme Court is the god not only of the judicial system but of the political and economic systems as well. Citizens of this country cannot in honesty claim to be under the Constitution. We are not "One Nation Under God." We are "One Nation Under the Supreme Court." The Supreme Court nine, who come to power by presidential appointment and not by popular election, govern this nation.

Fully cognizant of their god-function, the justices, garbed appropriately in black, flowing, priestly robes, legislate over life and death. They are deified when they pass away, and perpetuity is assured by ready replacements.

The Supreme Court initially was instituted, as Article III clearly states, to decide disputes of constitutional nature. Being in recent times dissatisfied with serving as lawgiver, it has usurped the legislative function of Congress. To function as god of the state, the Court must not only administer law, but make it.

But acting as god of this system is difficult when what constitute that god are fallen men. When man fell into sin, his intellect fell also. Men are limited, and when they step beyond their bounds they lose all perspective. Man, to put it simply, is not and cannot be God. Nor can he behave as the true God.

This being the case, the Court, disdaining absolutes, finds itself steeped in relativism and situational ethics. What is good in one instance can be bad in the next. Illegal today, murder, if the situation changes, may be legal tomorrow. Murder is, therefore, in the minds of the god of this system, relative.

Equally significant, the Court, as well as the legal mind in general, has been heavily influenced by the philosophy of men like Justice Oliver Wendell Holmes. Embracing Kantian philosophy, Holmes declared that law is not logic but experience only. In other words, as a blind man stumbles along the unknown corridors of life, he touches and feels his way along. This is the approach to law taken by the Supreme Court. Needless to say, this brings more than a little uncertainty onto the legal scene.

By 1962 the leaven of relativism had leavened the Supreme Court. To the Court God was dead, and His church was dead. All that remained was the task of disestablishing it.

The Counterreligion

Man, an inherently religious entity, must worship. No matter how vehemently man may try, he cannot gainsay this fact. Being religious, the creature man must exercise faith. At issue is: In what or whom shall he repose his faith? Wherever man is situated there will be religion, formal or informal.

Humanism is one such religion that requires faith and worship. For example, in 1971 a conscientious objector to the Vietnam War explained that he rested his religious objection to this unjust war "on the grounds of religious belief, specifically 'humanism.' This essentially means respect and love for man, faith in his inherent goodness and perfectibility, and confidence in his capability to improve some of the pains of the human condition."[2]

Faith here is defined in terms of man. Humanism denies original sin, holding that man is not depraved but possesses "inherent goodness and perfectibility." Man, humanism asserts, is evolving to a perfect state. He can "improve some of the pains of the human condition." Traditionally, this improvement of the human condition has come by way of government control through laws, bureaucratic planning, welfare, etc. The religion of humanism eventually finds its answer in the state or government, thereby deifying, in effect, the state. It becomes the messiah of the masses who continually cry out, "Feed us, wipe our tears."

From the cradle to the grave security is provided by the government. Most perplexing about all this is that as the government provides security, the people clamor for more and more benefits. And the more security government provides, the more control it gains. The more control it gains, the larger it becomes. The larger it becomes, the more power it possesses. The people glory in the government's power until the state begins turning on them. Fear sets in and ridicule of the state becomes the vogue. What people want is noninterference from their god while eating the state's cake. This is unrealistic.

The crucial point here is that now the people no longer seek the true God, but, instead, bow to the man-made god. Judgment from the true God will follow.

"You shall have no other gods besides me" (Exodus 20:3) is God's command. Man's own conception of divinity is prohibited. God has revealed Himself, and man is not to bow down to anything of his own making.

The God of Scripture is a jealous God. He intends to keep and protect that which is His. The humanistic god is a jealous god also. This man-made god requires sacrifice to itself only—anything sacrificed beyond that it abhors. On this premise, tax exemption for churches and other Christian organizations, which in the past was a sacrifice by the government to God, will in the near future be severely handicapped and eventually eliminated.

The established religion in this country is the state or government. Religion, it must be remembered, is never disestablished. Only a church can be disestablished. The aim of the religion of humanity, as is obvious, has for some years been the disestablishment of the Christian church.

Bogus Freedom *the advancement of Satan through denying our Lord*

The Christian should know that the only true freedom is in Jesus Christ. He specifically said that if "the Son shall make you free, you shall be free indeed" (John 8:36). The Scriptures demonstrate that if Christ has not freed you, then you are a slave to sin.

In the name of "freedom" the humanistic modern man continually seeks after human rights. The only practical source of rights for the humanist, however, is the government. Once the state grants rights, the state must ensure and enforce these rights. The state, or government, must increase in size and power to function as the guardian of freedom. More bureaucratic institutions are required to supervise and keep surveillance over the granted human rights. The humanist's quest eventually leads to the totalitarian state. *Communism taking wide sweeps as people turn from our Savior*

With each administration and with each march on Washington for human rights apart from God, the people are steadily building the "octogovernment." Its tentacles reach into every stream of life in seeking to control. Just as the Christian's God is omnipotent, omniscient, and omnipresent, the state as god seeks to be all-knowing. Witness the ever-growing data files and computer sheets that possess more detailed information about us than we ourselves could ever imagine. The state in order to assure the triumph of human rights must gain greater power over man.

The time is so short and I've committed my loved ones to His care without a single doubt. Anti Christ is about to arise

I'm so thankful for the Holy Spirit and the discernment, faith and detection, perseverence, God gives me.

Amidst the increasing power of the octogovernment the individual and individual rights gradually fade. In this country today the emphasis has shifted from individual rights to group rights. There is a group movement in every stratum of life.

The shift to the group accompanies the shift to the masses. The biblical Trinity is unified, and in imitation the state seeks unity. No longer are we men, but we are *man* and *mankind*. All is one. Disturbing the peace of the unity of the state is scorned upon. Men are made to believe there are no differences between them. They are one, and their god is the state. *take warning*

Christians must remember that we serve God, not mankind. When I hear a Christian say, "I'm doing this for mankind," I know he is in the wrong boat, a sinking boat at that. Joseph de Maistre, distressed at repeated allusions to mankind, put it well when he in 1875 said, "I have seen Frenchmen, Italians, Russians, but as for man, I declare I never met him in my life: if he exists, it's without my knowledge."

We can seek nothing apart from God and hope to win by it. The nation and its people who seek freedom apart from God will suffer judgment. The more often modern man seeks human rights, the less freedoms he really has. It's a vicious circle without fulfillment. The Rolling Stones epitomized modern man's dilemma well when they sang, "I can't get no satisfaction."

Out from Under

David in his prayer for forgiveness in Psalm 51 confessed, "Against thee, thee only, I have sinned...." The message here is that when men transgress the law of God, the sin is always directly against God and no other.

This particular concept has application to the state. In Romans 13 the state or government is clearly given only a *ministerial* function (the church's function is also ministerial). In other words, the state is to serve God by punishing the evildoer and by protecting the godly, thereby promoting good. Whenever the state fails to do that, it then comes under the wrath of God.

The height of insolence, however, occurs when the state clearly rejects God, making itself a god. The state has then stepped out from under its obligation of service and has assumed a function for which it was not designed.

It is God's sovereignty that is attacked in this situation. God is king over both the state and the church. He is sovereign over all the earth. There is nothing separate from Him except by illusion. God's power is always there, and His wrath hangs in the balance only to be exercised at the proper time. Man cannot escape God.

Romans 13 requires the Christian to be in "subjection to the governing authorities" because they "are established by God." Such subjection must be qualified. There are some situations in which the Christian is not to subject himself to the state. For instance, the Scriptures forbid subjection to the state if the latter requires the Christian to commit an ungodly act, if it interferes with worship, or if it by law debars the Christian from communicating the Gospel.

The Jews of Christ's day wanted a conquering messiah, but Jesus would not fit the bill. They wanted to overthrow Rome, but Jesus instructed them to pay Caesar his due. Victory was not to be by revolution.

Christ as well as Paul exhorts Christians to follow lawful means to air their grievances before the state. Christians eschew civil disobedience for the logic of civil disobedience is revolution. The need is not for revolution but for *regeneration*.

Subtle Persecution

Historically, there have been two major stages in the attack on religious liberty. First, the government and its entities are secularized in the name of freedom, and second, every prerogative or privilege of the church is attacked in an indirect manner so that, in disguised fashion, its right to exist is denied.[3]

In the name of freedom the United States, through its statist lawgiver, the Supreme Court, has nearly accomplished the secularization of the state. Interestingly the word *tyrant*, from the Greek *tyrannos*, literally means a secular ruler; one who rules without the sanction of a religious law, but with "an authority that was not derived from the worship, a power that religion had not established."[4] The secularized state is, in a word, a government not founded on Christian precepts, or biblical law, but, instead, premised on man-made laws.

The United States government has become so secularized and anti-God that even some of its highest officials abhor the mention of His name. When, for example, Henry Kissinger, then secretary of state, wed wife Nancy, he, and she, demanded that the word *God* be omitted during their wedding ceremony.

The trend toward secularization progresses according to the input of leftist or ultraliberal thought into the system. The more liberal the government, the more autonomous the government is from God. In his book *Leftism,* Erik von Kuehnelt-Leddihn concludes that as liberal thought enters the state system the result is either "complete hostile annexation of the church ('Josephinistic' establishments under state control) or persecution of the church by separation. Religion is then removed from the marketplace and the school, later from other domains of public life. The state will not tolerate any gods besides itself."[5]

As the government becomes more and more secularized, the privileges of the church are steadily chipped away so that in the end its very right to exist is denied. A primary potential mode of attack is denial of the church's tax-exemption status. As the Supreme Court itself has noted, "The power to tax is the power to destroy."

Revoking tax exemption is a way of placing the church under the complete domination of the state. If our government continues its present ultraliberal course, then denial of tax exemption to the church is the ultimate outcome. "To ask the church to render tribute unto Caesar is to deny that it has any direct approach to God, to declare, in essence, that the church's approach to God and man is mediated through the state."[6]

An area in which the church is now denied its prerogatives is that of planning commissions and zoning laws. Zoning laws radiate an aura of progress and civic improvement. They also have a basic appeal to the desire of people to improve their property (while steadily infringing their property rights). But through zoning laws countless churches have been denied building permits. Such denial of the right to exist for these churches has been upheld by the United States Supreme Court.[7]

This move against the organized institutional church has not been effective enough. Now the area of concentration is private residential Bible studies. For example, a 1976 decision by a federal district court in Virginia ruled that it was unconstitutional for parents to conduct Bible or religious-oriented classes in their own homes with their own children.[8] The decision was handed down on an appeal that began as a zoning case. A priest was charged with a zoning violation because he was conducting classes in private homes. Parents then began to conduct their own classes and were also charged with zoning violations. This all led to the district-court decision.

Tyranny, as was noted earlier, has its origin in secularism, a rule founded on man-made laws. Secularism is at bottom the religion of humanity. It is the most oppressive and dangerous of all cults because it sees no law beyond the state as a check against its lust for power.

In his quest to secularize his entire life man is attempting to be a god, thereby separating himself from the true God. But this is mere illusion. The grand promoter of this deception has to date been the Supreme Court. It is, however, merely an endeavor to disestablish the Christian church.

Undeniably, Christianity is being disestablished in the United States, thereby making way for the establishment of the religion of humanity. Every religion requires sacrifice and worship. When Satan tempted Christ he said, "All these things will I give you if you fall down and worship me." To such philosophy Jesus replied: "Be gone, Satan! For it is written, 'You shall worship the Lord your God, and serve him only' " (Matthew 4:9–10).

In Government We Trust

The true church of Christ proclaims the truths of the Scriptures. It gives man dignity, and also announces that there is but one true God who reigns over the earth. The message of Christianity is not only religious but political as well. The church disagrees that the state is god. It is at variance with the state on this issue.

It must be understood, however, that one religion cannot tolerate another religion. The religion in power must war against an opposing religion, or it will fade from the scene. The religion of humanity, therefore, has been warring against the Christian church and so far it has been successful in its attempts to disestablish the church.

The holy Scriptures strongly assert that man, to be free from the chains of sin, must receive the gift of Christ's salvation. This freedom in Christ leaves the Christian with total security in his future. His needs, the Bible promises, will be met by God.

The slave is the one who looks to his master for total security. The slave wants his master to provide food, clothing, and shelter for him. When he doesn't receive what he believes to be his quota, he pleads for relief.

The slave mentality has demanded that his god sacrifice to him. He asserts as a matter of right that his needs must be met. To paraphrase an old saying, "The world owes him a living."

The statist god, however, requires that the sacrifice be made to it. This sacrifice comes in varying forms, ranging from excessive taxation (with inflation being a form of tax) to relinquishment of individuality in the name of the state. The true freedom to give to the true God as one sees fit is lost by coercion and intervention of the government.

The slave mentality cannot accept freedom. Freedom means responsibility and work. Freedom is "a decent respect for the needs of others and a willingness to forgo unlimited self-assertion at the expense of others. Without this basic, freedom becomes meaningless; otherwise, the freedom of a few is won only by the subjugation of the many."[9] True freedom is under the law of God for without it freedom vanishes altogether.

Justice William Douglas of the Supreme Court was one such person who felt that unlimited self-assertion at the expense of others was something on which freedom was based. He believed it was wrong for this nation to bear the words "In God We Trust" on its coins. Douglas never said with what he would replace those words. But it takes little imagination to realize that one day soon the coins of this country may well be inscribed, "In Government We Trust." Not only would this satisfy the atheist, but it would soothe the slave mentality also. It would also be an honest description of the state of affairs in the United States today.

¿ 9 ⸙

The End?

*The people will fancy an appearance of freedom; illusion
will be their native land.*

Saint Just

One of the most influential books in recent years has been
Alvin Toffler's *Future Shock.*[1] His theory is that technology is
moving at such a pace man does not have a chance to adjust to it.
If and when man adjusts to an oncoming change, by this time
another altering effect is already converging on him. As disparaging
as the book may be, it succeeds in forcing us to face the fact that
the future is with us now and its problems are our problems in the
present.

Why is modern society facing this "technological and cultural
shock"? Basically, the answer lies in the attempts made by man to
build his ideal or "great society." Whenever and wherever man
has proceeded to construct a utopia on his own terms he has succeeded in persecuting his fellow man. This phenomenon is "the
separation illusion" because man cannot succeed apart from God,
for man's means are the ends of death.

Throughout the ages countless men, Christian and non-
Christian alike, have intimated that religion is the basis of a moral
society. Wherever this principle has been denied, terror and totalitarianism have resulted. As Benjamin Franklin said, "If men are
so wicked as we now see them *with religion,* what would they be
without it?"

The Three Temptations

The great Russian writer Fyodor Dostoevsky was a Christian. In his last novel, *The Brothers Karamazov*, he reviews three questions posed to Christ in the wilderness by Satan and illustrates how the church of his day had fallen for these very temptations.[2] The chapter was entitled "The Grand Inquisitor," after the inquisitions by the church of the thirteenth century and following.[3] During the inquisitions the church purged the system of what it believed to be heretics, resulting in the death of thousands.

It is appropriate to apply the same three temptations to the modern state. Since the modern governmental systems have taken on a religious aura, it seems neither fallacious nor presumptuous to assume that the temptations can apply to them.

Under the influence of God the Holy Spirit, Jesus was led into the wilderness where He fasted for forty days and forty nights, all the while being tempted by Satan. Satan's three questions revealed the entire future history of man. Moreover, they offered three symbols which reconciled all the irreconcilable strivings on earth of man the sinner.

Bread and Stones

Christ came into the world empty of this world's goods. He did bring the promise of salvation and freedom. Most men, however, fear and dread freedom because there has been nothing more difficult for man and society to bear than freedom.[4] Satan first tempted Christ by saying, "If you are the Son of God, command that these stones become bread" (Matthew 4:3). Christ could have turned the stones into bread, and men would have followed Him in multitudes. Instead, Christ did not want to deprive man of his freedom, for obedience bought with bread is not the spiritual freedom that Christ desired for man. Therefore, Christ replied, "It is written, 'Man shall not live on bread alone, but on every word that proceeds out of the mouth of God' " (Matthew 4:4).

Christ promised man heavenly bread, but man has sought earthly bread instead. "Enslave us, but feed us" is the cry of modern man.[5] Someday man might understand that freedom and assurance of daily bread are incompatible in a fallen world, but then it may be too late.

For the Love of Slavery

In the foreword to his futuristic novel, *Brave New World,* Aldous Huxley wrote that a "really efficient totalitarian state would be one in which the all-powerful executive of political bosses and their army of managers control a population of slaves who do not have to be coerced because they love their servitude. To make them love it is the task assigned, in present-day totalitarian states, to ministers of propaganda, newspaper editors, and school-teachers."[6]

Approximately a century ago, following his visit to America, Alexis de Tocqueville prophesied that if totalitarianism (tyranny) was established in a democratic state, it would have a different character than the old terror regimes. "It would," he said, "be more widespread and milder: it would degrade men rather than torment them."[7] And how are men degraded? In post-America the process of democratization (reducing every man to the eye level of every other man) is producing a commune, not a society of individuals. This not only lowers the superior individual, but also prevents the less fortunate from ever rising any higher. A general degradation of the culture is the result. *Communist Ideology*

Another method of degrading man occurs when he loses his one true satisfaction in life—fulfillment through work. As man is replaced by machine and is retired on a guaranteed income he begins dying inside. Like the contemporary aged man who retires and on the average dies three years later, modern man is faced with a similar degradation.

The goal of the totalitarian government, according to Huxley, is to feed the people by becoming the great provider. The "provider state" is administered by the government that is in the business of turning stones to bread. In this way the government gains the obedience of the people.

As the people gain more and more from their god, the state, they ask for more. For example, the United States has evolved from assistance check payments to a new clamoring for a guaranteed income.

There is always a catch, however, when one deals with a government administered apart from God. As the state gives more, it takes more in return. The United States is taxing the individual citizen at a phenomenal rate to support its welfare system. Sweden, the "ideal" welfare state, extracts eighty-five percent from the paycheck, with some individuals paying over one hundred percent in taxes.[8]

There is no such thing as getting something for nothing from the state that has established itself as the ultimate order. Like all gods, it requires that a sacrifice be made to it. The sacrifice it requires is indeed a most precious item—freedom.

The Illusion of Freedom

B. F. Skinner believes that to tame the animal nature in man, man must be deprived of his value, dignity, worth, and freedom. Skinner opts for positive control of man's behavior rather than negative control. For example, instead of using punishment as an effective statist control to keep the people from defecting, a better method for the government to pursue would be to make life more interesting. To Skinner, life is made more interesting by providing *bread,* circuses, sports, gambling, the use of alcohol and other drugs, and various kinds of sexual behavior.[9] He quotes the Goncourt brothers, who wrote about the rise of pornography in the France of their day: "Pornographic literature serves a Bas-Empire . . . one tames a people as one tames lions, by masturbation."[10]

Skinner notes that under the type of system evolving in the United States, the entire population eventually becomes a slave population. By means of positive control the people become slaves without knowing it.

Skinner scorns the literature of freedom because it makes man aware of his slavery while failing to rescue him from his unhappiness.[11] "Happiness," to Skinner, is more important than freedom. Why not, if men are compared to a herd of animals? Without freedom, however, there is no happiness. Huxley recognized this when he said it was important that "the great societies" provide frequent vacations for the citizens in order for them to escape all the "happiness."

The real threat to freedom is a system of slavery so well designed that it does not breed revolt. A system which does not breed revolt will be a state that is a master of manipulation.

A particularly important statist mode of keeping revolt down is to give the people choices, thereby maintaining an appearance of freedom. The choices presented to the people, however, are totally dictated by the government. Actually, freedom in the true sense of the word is destroyed when this occurs. Why? A clever government will only present a group of options, any of which, if chosen, will be most desirable to it.

Rousseau said that there is no subjugation so perfect as that which keeps the appearance of freedom because it captures man's ability willfully to choose and act. In other words, a rat in a maze does not possess choices, only alternatives.

To have the ability and duty to choose requires responsibility, and this modern man is running away from. Responsibility is an aspect of freedom, thereby making freedom a burden to an irresponsible populace. As the grand inquisitor said to Christ, "Have you forgotten that peace, and even death, is more attractive to man than freedom of choice ... there is nothing more alluring to man than freedom of conscience, but neither is there anything more agonizing."[12]

Jacques Ellul, remarking on what he calls the "illusion of freedom," said the government that talks most about freedom denies it most.[13] If a citizenry is truly free, then why does the president or leader in every speech tell it how free it is. A people truly free needs not to be told it is.

Hollow Freedom

Aleksandr Solzhenitsyn, the Nobel Prize–winning Russian expatriate, is a Christian who once believed the West was the bastion of freedom. He has now grown sour in his views toward Western democracy. Basically, Solzhenitsyn says that as morality declines freedom declines. Of course, the decline of morality is the decline of the effectiveness of Christianity to direct the culture.

In his controversial BBC interview in late 1975, Solzhenitsyn shocked Great Britain when he said the moral consciousness of the Western nations had descended so low that the Soviet Union didn't need weapons to conquer the West. All it needed, he said, was its bare hands.

"Genuinely human freedom," declared Solzhenitsyn, "is inner freedom given to us by God: freedom to decide upon our own acts, as well as moral responsibility for them."[14] This inner freedom is denied by a manipulative government that takes away man's responsibility for his acts by charging that all he does wrong is caused by the environment. From this, B. F. Skinner says control the environment and man is controlled.

As opposed to Solzhenitsyn's inner freedom, what type of freedom do we have? Says Solzhenitsyn:

> *Freedom! to litter compulsorily with commercial rubbish the mail boxes, the eyes, ears, and brains of the people, the telecasts—so that it is impossible to watch a single one with a sense of coherence. Freedom! to impose information taking no account of the right of the individual not to accept it, of the right of the individual to peace of mind. Freedom! to spit in the eye and in the soul of the passerby and the passenger with advertising.... Freedom! for editors and film producers to start the younger generation off with seductive miscreations. Freedom! for adolescents of 14–18 years to immerse themselves in idleness and amusements instead of invigorating tasks and spiritual growth.... Freedom! for healthy young adults to avoid work and live at the expense of society.... Freedom! for politicians indiscriminately to bring about whatever pleases the voter today, but not what farsightedly provides for his safety and well-being.*[15]

Solzhenitsyn is speaking of a destructive freedom—one that adds chains to men instead of fulfillment. It is a freedom to act and speak regardless of the rights of others. Most of all, it is a freedom from God and His law, which is no freedom at all.

Like the hollow men of T. S. Eliot's epic poem, the word *freedom* has become "filled with straw." It has no content for it is hollow freedom. When man seeks freedom from God, freedom then becomes "another word for nothing else to lose."

Man cannot live on bread alone, and when he attempts to, his bread is taken away in the end. Ultimately, his life is also taken by the state.

God or Satan?

Following Jesus' renunciation of Satan's first temptation, the great deceiver led Him to a mountaintop and showed Him all the kingdoms of the world "in a moment of time" (Matthew 4:8; Luke 4:5). Satan then said to Christ, "All these things will I give to you, if you fall down and worship me" (Matthew 4:9).

The temptation to serve something other than the true God has plagued man throughout history. Men have often attempted to serve the true God and something else at the same time. Israel tried this repeatedly. But Christ made it clear in the Sermon on the Mount that man cannot serve two masters simultaneously (Matthew 6:24).

Those About to Die

In the Roman games the gladiators of the arena paraded before the assembled multitude while a fifty-piece band played a march. As the gladiators came to the emperor's private box, they stopped, raised their right hands (similar to the Nazi salute), and chanted, "Hail, Caesar! We who are about to die salute you."[16] The angel Gabriel appeared before the virgin Mary in Nazareth of Galilee and declared, "Hail, thou that are highly favored, the Lord is with thee; blessed are thou among women" (Luke 1:28). Both salutations were religious.

From the early days of Rome, the Roman games were a basic religious practice of the state. Accordingly, Pierre Grimal said, "Their religious character is undeniable."[17] In these two salutes to deity there is set forth symbolically the battle of the centuries— Christ versus Caesar, or man under God versus man under the state or government.

As head of the Roman college of priests, the emperor Augustus Caesar gave the masses of the Roman Empire forgiveness for their past sins. Augustus was looked upon as a messiah and savior. An inscription on Roman coins even hailed him as the "son of god."[18]

The conflict between the two rivals was inescapable. In the early part of the first century Simon Peter, apostle of Jesus Christ, challenged the religious and civil leaders of his day, declaring, "There is salvation in no one else; for there is no other name under heaven that has been given among men, by which we must be saved" (Acts 4:12). The issue was now clear. The battle was not between church and state, but between two kingdoms declaring ultimate and divine authority over all men.

Eventually, the Christians within Rome were ordered by the government to burn incense to the superior jurisdiction of the state. To acquiesce meant that they recognized the earthly government had superior jurisdiction over man as against God. The early Christians refused to acknowledge Caesar's claim and pledged allegiance to none other than Christ. As a result, they were horribly persecuted for their loyalty to God.

Seeking the Anthill

Christ repulsed Satan's temptation to worship him by replying, "Be gone, Satan! For it is written, 'You shall worship the Lord your God, and serve him only' " (Matthew 4:10). The secular governments have accepted what Christ rejected, but they have been thwarted from ruling all the kingdoms of the earth. The great conquerors Alexander the Great and Genghis Khan failed to gain the whole.

The new tower of Babel, however, is now coming into view. Man is attempting to unite in a harmonious anthill where there are no dissenting voices. There is an almost unquenchable thirst in man to find the ultimate unity. Christ rejected this temptation; He knew that fallen man, to accomplish unity, would have to serve the author of evil.

The United Nations is an attempt to find the solution to the dispersion that God caused to fall upon man after Nimrod had vaulted to power. The United Nations is now focusing on the promise of youth. It has established at the cost of $11.5 million an international school that is teaching a future elite how to rule the world.[19] Children numbering 1,431 from 101 nations are being taught what is essentially the politics of a unified world.[20] Most of these children will be the leaders or influential officials of their countries in twenty years or less. The answer is seen as unity, not regeneration through salvation.

There is nothing a man is more anxious to do than find something to worship. It must unquestionably be something that all men can agree to worship communally, however. A call is going out at the present time for a world government and a leader to assume control of the earth.

Christ rejected the immense power He would hold if He both fed and controlled men's consciences. Jesus acknowledged it was

God's sovereignty that was over man and that there could be only death within the separation illusion. He knew where the answer to man's dilemma was centered, and it was not in hopes of a world government.

Tempting God

There are three forces on earth that can overcome and capture once and for all the conscience of man and give him pseudohappiness. These are miracles, authority, and mystery.[21] Christ rejected the first, the second, and finally the third in order to set an example for man.

When Satan laid his last temptation on Jesus it was aimed not only at Christ but at God the Father also. The dreaded spirit led Him to Jerusalem and set Him on the pinnacle of the temple, saying, "If you are the Son of God, throw yourself down; for it is written, 'He will give His angels charge concerning you; and, on their hands they will bear you up, lest you strike your foot against a stone' " (Matthew 4:6).

Acting like the God He is, Christ answered, "It is written, 'You shall not tempt the Lord your God' " (Matthew 4:7). Christ would not test God for this would show that He had lost His faith in the Father.

Man has not withstood this temptation. The grand inquisitor asked Christ, "Didn't you know that whenever man rejects miracles he rejects God, because he seeks not so much God as miracles?"[22] Man cannot live without miracles so he creates his own. He turns to astrology, sorcery, witchcraft, and pseudo-Christianity even though he is an atheist, heretic, or agnostic.

As it denies God the state assumes the role of the miracle worker. It feeds and clothes its citizens from cradle to grave with statist services. Faith is transferred from the true God to the statist god, and government now takes on the aura of "Government" with a capital G.

The charismatic political leader who, shrouded with mystery, announces he will cure all ills is an example of the modern miracle worker. People follow the contemporary leader less for what he can offer in the way of godliness and leadership than for what he can offer in the way of expanded governmental services. Offering "God without God" to the people, they rush to the polls to elect him. The mistrust of his predecessor is soon forgotten because, as Ellul says, modern man "is a man without memory."[23]

Christ would not come down when they taunted Him and challenged Him, saying, "Let Him now come down from the cross, and we shall believe in Him" (Matthew 27:42). Christ's way of saving men was not by curiosity-pleasing power displays. He required love from redeemed hearts "rather than the servile rapture of slaves subdued forever by a display of power."[24]

The mighty show of power by the modern police state which controls by coercion is in contrast to the modern provider state that is literally destroying its people with irresponsibility. Christ would not buy man's love or dazzle him with miracles in order to control him. He was honest, but they crucified Him. What was His crime? He so loved sinful men that He gave them the terrible gift of freedom from sin.

Neutralization

In his song "Story of Isaac" Leonard Cohen wrote, "Thought I saw an eagle, but it might have been a vulture. I never could decide."[25] Many people in the United States today are undecided on the same issue: has the American eagle become a vulture?

Remember, the Roman Empire was not overthrown; it committed suicide. It collapsed like a deflated balloon because it had decayed from within. Internal breakdown and the lack of quality people have been the historical results of governments that have fallen prey to the three satanic temptations. Initially, everything is democratized or reduced to equality by coercion. Initiative is stifled, thereby giving the state control over a docile citizenry. The people in effect become neutralized and tragically servile.

When the barbarians entered the Roman senate, they listened to an orator proposing a plan to stop them if they should invade Rome. Some of the invaders poked the sitting Roman senators to see if they were alive because they looked like statues. The senators had become neutralized by a decaying society.

Those with a sense of responsibility fought against the spirit of decay in Rome. Theaters, games, and festivals were organized in an unprecedented number while grain, wine, and money were distributed.[26] Likewise, the coins were struck with words of encouragement.[27] Answers were sought from everyone except God. Meanwhile, the German tribes were smashing through the Roman lines, and the old order was tottering to an end.

All one has to do is look around at what is happening in the United States to see the parallel between decaying Rome and post-America. The decay is gnawing at the vitals of the country. The eagle looks more like a vulture these days.

A Fading Constitution

The post-American federal government has become a monolithic snail gradually consuming all it touches. As a Republic founded on law, America could become centralized and controlled by the federal government only through a change in the law. The basic legal foundation of the American Republic was the Constitution. It was a conservative document, basically antichange in nature, and its stalwartness to alteration is to be admired.

The post-American Supreme Court has taken up Caesar's sword and has interpreted the Constitution away. The Court, therefore, has become the major source of change in the structure of the United States government because it is at this level that laws are approved or disapproved.

One can respond plaintively: But we have more laws than we've ever had. Are not we still a government of laws? We are still a government of laws, but relativistic philosophy has eroded the original intent of many of these laws. The United States is still grounded on law but is subject to capricious change by the courts. This country has more laws than ever before, but it also has more corruption than ever before. As Tacitus recognized early in man's history, "The more corrupt the government, the greater the number of laws."

History illustrates that as law and order decline, chaos and anarchy set in. As this occurs someone emerges similar to Plato's philosopher–king, who takes total control to establish order. But order is established in a lawless society by tyranny. And the worst type of tyranny is the kind that builds the totalitarian state gradually so that few are really aware of what is happening. When the populace awakens to reality, it either is apathetic or finds itself helpless to resist.

No Private Domain

A major step in any central government's attempt to create a totalitarian state is to deprive the citizen completely of his privacy. Pornography is allowed to run roughshod, for one reason, because it exposes the most intimate and secret moments to the public mind. Sex then becomes a debased and filthy thing instead of a healthy gift for procreation and private enjoyment.

The government eventually declares that there is no private domain. Democratization requires that all be made known so that none is more equal than any other. Any attempts to create a private domain separate from the public domain are, therefore, scorned upon.   *Dear God — deliver. Come quickly*

The Supreme Court took a giant step toward eradicating the private domain in a 1976 decision that held that private schools may not legally close their doors to properly qualified black children because of race.[28] This case, in effect, says that there is no such thing as private education, only public education.

The gist of the case was that the freedom-of-contract language of the 1866 Civil Rights Act required private schools to enter into contracts with blacks eligible for admission if the schools contracted with white families whose children were similarly qualified.[29] The Court ignored the constitutional argument that the schools were being denied freedom to contract with whomever they chose. The freedom of contract, however, has been a fundamental liberty in the United States since the founding of the Republic.

I believe that a private school that discriminates on the basis of race is wrong, but it is the school's right under the Constitution of the United States Republic. Blacks have a reason to be upset at a private school that excludes them because of their race, but this is not the dominating issue. What we are more concerned with here is the right of private schools to remain private.

John Jay, the first chief justice of the Supreme Court, said, "The people who own the country ought to govern it." He is talking about private ownership as opposed to public dominance. Jay saw the private domain as essential to liberty. It is paramount to all men, whether they be black, red, or white, that the tide of centralizing control be turned back. If not, all races will be absorbed into the state grinder.

The Warring Kingdoms

The birth of Christ, God born into the world, brought to a head the issue of who has jurisdiction over man—the government or God. As it was in the era of the Caesars, so today this issue has become an arena of both spiritual and physical warfare.

In the case discussed above, the Supreme Court emphasized that it was withholding judgment on the legality of private schools that limited enrollments to members of one sex or religious faith.[30] In addition, the Court said it was leaving open the question of whether church-related schools that excluded blacks because of their members' religious tenets would eventually have to become public.[31]

The Supreme Court will usually not decide an issue unless that issue is argued before it, and that is why the Court did not rule on Christian schools and discrimination according to religious belief. If, however, that issue is sued upon and the Court is consistent with its reasoning in the case above, then private Christian schools will not be able to exclude other religions or even atheists.

Recently the issue of "no private domain" reached frightening proportions in Ohio. At stake was the survival of Christian education. The Tabernacle Christian School, a private Christian elementary school in Bradford, Ohio, was operating without having applied for a charter from the state and without having submitted a plan showing the total school organization and program. An independent school that refused state or federal money, Tabernacle had been built solely by donations from private individuals. Consequently, the state of Ohio refused to give it accreditation.

Twelve parents of children enrolled in and attending the school were indicted by a county grand jury for violating an Ohio state law, which provided that it was a criminal violation for a parent to fail to send his or her child to a state-accredited school. In the process the county decided to term the children "neglected minor children," thereby giving the state the power to remove the children from their parents and place them in foster homes. The foster parents would then have the duty to return the children to the public schools.

The case finally went to court, and in mid-1976 the Ohio Supreme Court ruled in favor of the Christian families who were being persecuted.[32] Many states had been watching this case closely, perhaps to see what move they should make next against Christian education.

Many Christian parents also moved to strike out an Ohio law that subordinates the parents' "natural rights" of custody and control to the state government in providing education for the child. The issue, again, is that there is to be no private domain because the government seeks total jurisdiction over man, thereby challenging the right of God to have that jurisdiction.

The New States of America

The Center for the Study of Democratic Institutions, upon a grant of $15 million from the Ford Foundation, has drafted a new "constitution." Six years in the making, this document was sired by a tax-exempt organization composed of officials who are not only not elected, but more than a little audacious to take to themselves the task of writing a new constitution. Very few people even know that this organization exists because it has been made known to only a select group of influential citizens. In 1974 the final version of the constitution emerged, entitled "Constitution of the New States of America."[33]

Of special interest to Christians is Article I, Section 8, which reads, "The practice of religion shall be privileged; but no religion shall be imposed by some on others, and none shall have public support."[34] This section is aimed at reducing Christianity to the level of all other religions (democratization), making it thereby as unimportant as other "routes to God." Section 8 could also be utilized effectively to restrict Christians in their attempts to evangelize and spread the Gospel. In addition, it states that no religion "shall have public support." Tax exemption for religious organizations would, therefore, be illegal, as most non-Christians reason, because it is "indirect" public support of religion.

Article I, Section 10 reads: "Those who cannot contribute to productivity shall be entitled to a share of the national product; but distribution shall be fair and the total may not exceed the amount for this purpose held in the National Sharing Fund."[35] This section is an attempt to usher in pure democracy as well as what Peter F. Drucker has called "the unseen revolution," which is socialism.[36]

Man becoming God's purity & love being
replaced by a pure Democracy of communism
which means a take over of the Anti Christ

Section 10 would require that a portion of all wages go into a public sharing fund, and those who did not work would be entitled to a fair share. This would in essence require forced labor and coerced sharing. Individual initiative would be stifled—the same individualism and confidence that were exhibited "by Renaissance Florence, Elizabethan England, and the America of the Founding Fathers."[37] The result would be the same total socialism that has led to the governmental crisis in Sweden.

Article I, Part B, Section 8 provides for the power of violence to be centralized in the government: "There shall be a responsibility to avoid violence and to keep peace; for this reason the bearing of arms or the possession of lethal weapons shall be confined to the police, members of the armed forces and those licensed under law."[38] This section is a direct repudiation of the Second Amendment to the present Constitution, which amendment provides that "the right of the people to keep and bear arms, shall not be infringed." Current crusaders for gun control fail to recognize that guns are not inherently bad. It is the men pulling the triggers who need to be controlled, and the only way in a free society that man can be effectively controlled is through regeneration, not coercion.

In a day when terrorists are running rampant, this is dangerous legislation. Terrorists will always have guns, and no one wants to be rendered defenseless against a maniac who believes he is a mini-god.[39]

Finally, Article 12, Section 5 reads in part: "For establishing New States' boundaries a commission of thirteen, appointed by the President, shall make recommendations within one year."[40] When this was written, Richard Nixon had already undertaken to establish new boundaries for the United States when he signed Executive Order 11647 in February 1972. The presidential decree divided the fifty states into ten "federal regional councils." This was designed to let the people exist in the old framework while newly emerging regional governments gradually siphon off local power and pass it on to the central government. Local entities, like cities, must under this executive order apply directly to the regional center for federal aid and assistance, bypassing their state government and elected officials in Washington, D.C.

For years the United States Supreme Court has discarded the history behind the framing of the Constitution and the intentions of the framers. Once a solid rock, the Constitution has become a bed of quicksand. It is not that we need a new constitution; the real need is to follow the old Constitution. If we can't do that, then a new constitution is in order, but the tyranny that emanates from the constitution proposed above must be avoided. If not, a totalitarian regime lurks around the corner.

1984 or Brave New World?

Two oracles of doom have passed into folklore which provide man with a view of the prison he seems bent on erecting around himself with the most disastrous ingenuity. Aldous Huxley's *Brave New World* was first published in 1932 and George Orwell's *Nineteen Eighty-Four* hit the market in 1949. Time has shown that both were written with great insight.

Both books foretell what is now apparent—that science is producing a new elitist ruling class that possesses overwhelming power. Both prophesy that man will eventually be completely controlled by a strange and revolutionary hybrid of technological manipulator and political manager. "But although the end in both cases is roughly the same," says Roland Huntford in *The New Totalitarians, "Brave New World* seems more applicable to the West at this time."[41] *Nineteen Eighty-Four* describes the logical conclusion of Communistic dictatorship, whereas *Brave New World* portrays the final corruption of the Western way of life.

Orwell postulates a reign of terror as a basis for establishing the control of the new ruling class. Huxley, on the other hand, supposes that scientific advances will bring the ruling class to power. Key to Huxley's hypothesis is that the new rulers will induce a gradual change in the people's mentality and in their acceptability of the scientific class, making physical coercion unnecessary. In other words, Huxley predicts that through a slow process man will come to serve a scientific class that all the while is manipulating him.

Man in the brave new world would move from the worship of God or even of man himself to the worship of technology. The victory of technology over man, Huxley showed, requires a highly centralized totalitarian government—a state that controls all in its totality. "There is no reason," he wrote, "why the new totalitarian should resemble the old. Government by firing squads ... is not merely inhumane ... it is demonstrably inefficient, and in an age of advanced technology, inefficiency is a sin against the Holy Ghost. A really efficient totalitarian state would be one in which the all-powerful executive of political bosses and their army of managers control a population of slaves who do not have to be coerced because they love their servitude."[42]

There are a number of reasons why man will love his servitude, or better, slavery. One reason would be that man would not really have the choice to serve. Humanist Albert Rosenfeld enthusiastically wrote,

> Imagine a dictator with a subject population—the dictator, a man who is sure he knows what is best for everyone; for himself, absolute power, for his subjects, happiness. He has at his command all the electrochemical techniques necessary for controlling the human brain as well as the most advanced methods for controlling human reproduction. He can have entire populations raised "artificially" without resorting to sex or family structure. He can also, if he chooses, have electrodes planted in the brains of his subjects, or begin administering "mind drugs" routinely, at a very early age.[43] *ushering in the Anti-Christ*

The brave new world envisioned by Huxley depends on economic security, for the love of servitude is impossible without it. Economic security alone is not sufficient; also needed are a hatred of individuality, an instinct for the collective life, a suspicion of parliamentary institutions, a worship of the state, and a preference for government by bureaucrat rather than politician.[44]

Essential to the brave new world and the love of slavery are the following discoveries and inventions: first, a technique of infant conditioning and mental suggestion aided by drugs; second, total control by the government manager over each person, enabling him to assign the people their proper places in the system; third, a peace-oriented society, one substituting for alcohol and other narcotics something less harmful and "more pleasure-giving than gin or heroin" (marijuana?); and fourth, a foolproof system of eugenics designed to standardize the production of test-tube babies.[45]

The gradual take over of all Individuals & people who do not obey and follow Christ. It promises liberty & life not slavery

The Synthesized Man

The horror of Nietzsche's crude remark, in his book *Thus Spake Zarathustra*, that "Dead are all Gods; now we desire the superman to live" is surfacing as a present-day reality. The day of the synthesized man is here. It is not surprising, therefore, that man–machine hookups are becoming very much a reality and that cybernetics (the study of the relationship between computers and the human nervous system) is thriving.[46]

One scientist has coined the term *dybology* (from the Hebrew word *dybbuk* meaning "unassigned soul").[47] Dybology defines the growing area between biology and engineering that can't be classified as being strictly biology or strictly engineering.[48] These "unassigned souls" would basically be life-mimicking mechanisms.

Many scientists now assert that the human body can be run cybernetically or, in other words, that it can be automated. In fact, experiments are currently being conducted in which men are wired to computers.

The proposed automated man is called a *cyborg*, which is short for cybernetic organism.[49] Supposedly, the cyborg would still be deemed a human being, although most might find it difficult to regard him as one after such radical tampering.

The cyborg is the coming superman that science has sought for decades to construct. Modern man in reality has lost the zealous faith he once placed in evolution. Now the evolutionist doesn't know if evolution will produce the man he desires. Therefore, science will have to create the superman.

The cyborg implies a thorough modification of the human body. For example, a cyborg designed for astronautics (space travel) would "resemble" a man "but an unearthly one indeed."[50] He would be sealed in a skintight suit, needing no pressurization because his lungs would be partially collapsed and the blood in them cooled down. Respiration and other bodily functions would be carried on for him cybernetically by small artificial organs and sensors—some of them attached to the outside of his body and some implanted surgically. Cyborgs would communicate with each other by having electrical impulses from their vocal cords transmitted by radio.[51] All bodily processes and activities of the cyborg would be controlled by computer.

All of this may sound like a "Star Trek" adventure, but the fact that NASA has invested money for research into the development of cyborgs indicates the seriousness with which these possibilities are being pursued.[52]

Experiments are also being conducted in which human beings are connected to a computer that induces action by the individual. In one experiment involving electrostimulation of the brain (ESB), the computer actually places a thought, or series of thoughts, into the mind of the person hooked to it. The startling phenomenon here is that the person believes he is originating the thought when actually the machine is doing the thinking.

The fusion of man and machine is synthesis which is designed to create a new man. The new man, however, is an automaton whose every act is dictated to him by way of computer. Not only is this type of scientific experimentation dangerous; it is also deadly.

People are becoming "synthetic." Artificial masks cover their sad faces. They have no purpose and meaning. *Synthetic* by its very meaning is unreal. Men who seek to be synthetic are denying that they are people. The synthetic man has no value. He can be grown in a test tube and taught by a computer. Waste no man-hours on him. The human fetus can be aborted because man is "junk."

French biologist Dr. Jean Rostard has asserted that with the advent of test-tube babies, "It will be little more than a game to change the subject's sex, the color of the eyes, the general proportions of body and limbs, and perhaps the facial features."[53] He also added that the "man-forming biologist might well be tempted to tamper with the intellectual makeup of the subject as well."[54] This is predestination, a la Huxley's *Brave New World,* of the behavior and attitudes of an individual for a lifetime.

Television in Totalitaria

The Swedes have shown us that relatively crude indoctrination by television and public education holds tremendous possibilities, provided only that there is effective centralized control of both.[55] Modern men are beginning to feel the strain of the unmanageability of their lives. With this hopelessness they seem to be surrendering "their civil liberties to increasingly authoritarian regimes that can explain the world to them anew."[56] As William Irwin Thompson puts it, "When the individual's consciousness is made up of a moving collage of televised fragments, his state of anxiety makes him prey to 'the recollectivization through terror' of the fascist state."[57] Therefore, helpless before the monster of electronics he has created, man in an act of faith surrenders to the power of explanation given him by way of television commentary. Like Mary Shelley's *Frankenstein*, man's "creation" apart from God is turning on him, and in the end it may very well destroy all mankind.

For the past twenty-five years industry and its advertisers have promoted through television the "pursuit of pleasure" as a substitute for the pursuit of happiness.[58] Pleasure has a way of controlling its seeker until in the end the seeker becomes a slave to something he can never attain in pleasure—happiness.

The Swedes through the medium of television have also demonstrated a kind of powerful semantic manipulation, not unlike Orwell's Newspeak, in which words are more or less gradually changed to mean something else.[59] In this way undesirable concepts can be done away with. The word *freedom* does not yet in Swedish mean exactly "slavery." It does, however, already imply "submission," thereby being effectively neutralized as a power-word in the vocabulary of forces that oppose servitude to the state.[60]

The End?

As in B. F. Skinner's elitist state, man in the brave new world has no worth or dignity; therefore, first abortion and then euthanasia are legalized. With approximately twenty percent of the population expected to be sixty-five years and older by the year 2030, euthanasia looms as a horrible remedy for a world already seeking ways to curb overpopulation.[61] The Supreme Court has recognized that people over fifty years of age have little worth in the work force.[62] What will the totalitarian state do with fifty million people who have nothing to do but consume precious food and energy needed by the young?

We cannot dismiss the state of "Totalitaria" as a problem to worry about in the future. It is banging at the door right now, causing some to question whether this is "the terminal generation."[63]

The separation illusion has caused man to believe than he can work apart from God and be free, but it is evident he is powerless to build utopia. Instead of utopia, men in the past have consistently built states of terror.

"The" Solution and "the" Hope

The solutions to the problems of mankind are provided in the Scriptures. The solutions have always been and always will be rooted in God's sovereignty. What may seem to be a problem to us may not be viewed as such by God. In other words, all things work together to effectuate His purpose.

If this is so, then what do the Scriptures offer in the way of hope for the post-American dilemma? Christ, speaking to the Christians, said, "You are the salt of the earth; but if the salt has become tasteless, how will it be made salty again? It is good for nothing any more, except to be thrown out and trampled under foot by men" (Matthew 5:13). Salt in Christ's day was utilized as a preservative (especially for meat). Christians, He says, are to have a flavoring and preservative influence upon the world. If not, then the salt "is good for nothing."

In order for the Christian people to have a preservative effect on the world (or this country), they must, as Francis Schaeffer said, take charge of the cultural direction. This means that wherever a Christian finds himself he must, as God's viceregent, control that particular area for God. To direct anything one must be in control of it. In other words, as commanded by God, the regenerate man is to subdue the earth (Genesis 1:28). To be sure, the Fall has affected this command but only in that it will take more sweat by regenerate man to accomplish God's purpose.

As intimated in chapter one, Christians must stop thinking of Christianity as a subculture. This is the logics of impotence. To be a preservative the regenerate man must be the dominant cultural influence, even as salt, to preserve meat, must cover it completely, not just partially.

To be a preservative of his culture, the true Christian must "judge the righteous judgment" (John 7:24). Judging a righteous judgment requires regeneration of the judge. Once regenerate, the Christian has the only source which affords him the ability to judge the world—the holy Scriptures. The apostle Paul writes, "He who is spiritual appraises all things, yet he himself is appraised by no man" (I Corinthians 2:15). Why? The regenerate man has "the mind of Christ" (I Corinthians 2:16). Put otherwise, if Christians take the Scriptures seriously, and if God is for them, who can stand against them?

Christ at the cross redeemed fallen man by substantially healing him so that as regenerate man he could take charge of the cultural direction. This means applying the Scriptures to every area of life because the "word of the cross ... is the power of God" (I Corinthians 1:18). Of course, the non-Christian will resist since the Scriptures are to him foolishness (I Corinthians 1:18, 21). Regenerate man, however, if properly versed, will turn foolishness into the wisdom of God, which will in turn eventually set the Christian in "the" place of authority.

Misinterpretation of Scripture and misunderstanding as to the Christian role in the world system have led to the failure of Christianity to preserve the sole faith in the American culture. If the faith had been preserved, then the system would not be facing destruction as it is today.

Christ commanded regenerate man to go "and make disciples of all the nations" (Matthew 28:19). The Lord is in effect saying, "Take affirmative action in my name and in the process you will control the nations." This is how the system is preserved.

Proverbs 9:10 clearly instructs us that unregenerate man has neither wisdom nor understanding. It remains to the Christian to provide that wisdom and understanding. For this the Christian must control the system.

In a country where there is more freedom to speak the gospel, there is a correspondingly higher duty on the Christian to take charge of the cultural direction of that country. The Christians in the Soviet Union must simply do the best they can. Christians in the United States, however, must do much more.

God abhors the thought of the Christian man who bows before the unregenerate man. He proclaims, "A righteous man falling down before the wicked is as a troubled fountain, and a corrupt spring" (Proverbs 25:26, KJV). The regenerate man cannot compromise, and there are situations in which Christians "ought to obey God rather than men" (Acts 5:29).

Although Romans 13:1-7 holds that Christians must submit to the government, this does not mean that they should accomplish the work of the wicked. The government is an institution divinely given to protect the good and punish the evil. As a ministry of God, government is prophetically to apply the gospel of Christ to its own sphere. Ungodly government more or less fails to carry out its proper function. Such government may be legitimate, but not everything it does is legitimate. The state is not above moral condemnation. The apostle Paul said, "I appeal to Caesar" (Acts 25:11). Are Christians to do less?

The call from God is for a Christian reformation. The basic foundation of a reformation is regeneration. Christians must take the gospel to every crack and crevice of this ungodly nation. This means not only joining the battle, but manning the front lines.

Should our country be regenerated and discipled for Christ, then everything it does must be founded on the holy Scriptures. As John Warwick Montgomery wrote, "The Christian heritage upon which our country was founded is ... a conviction that God's scriptural Word is the only proper basis for national hope."[64]

Once the family, the school, the government, etc., are founded upon the propositional revelation that God has given to man in the Scriptures, then the house is founded no longer upon quicksand, but, instead, upon a rock of granite.

If regenerate man can command his culture and country, then true freedom will reign, for Christ is the only source of freedom for man. In fact, He is the solution! If Christianity cannot do this, then I must be truthful in saying that the end is just around the corner.

A Twist of Fate

Puritan Jonathan Edwards was without doubt one of the greatest Christian thinkers this country has ever known. He has been deemed responsible for igniting the sparks that kindled the mid-eighteenth-century conflagration in America called the Great Awakening. Early in the Great Awakening Edwards said:

> *America has received the true religion of the old Continent.... And inasmuch as that Continent [Europe] has*

crucified Christ, they shall not have the honor of communicating religion in its most glorious state to us, but we to them ... when God is about to turn the earth into a Paradise, He does not begin His work where there is some good growth already, but in a wilderness, where nothing grows ... that the light may shine out of darkness, and the world be replenished from emptiness.

I believe Edwards' statement here drives the star-spangled nail into the coffin. As he said, America had inherited Christianity and as a result God had glorified Himself by building a Christian nation virtually *ex nihilo.*

If there is going to be a Christian reformation, then it will very likely occur not in a country "where there is some good growth already, but in a wilderness, where nothing grows." Why? God seeks to make Himself known, and the best way to glorify Himself is to make the light shine where only darkness prevails.

There "is some good growth already" in post-America, but most of the world is a wilderness without the gospel. The United States has had its chance and, as Francis Schaeffer makes clear in *Death in the City,* post-America is already under the judgment of God.

Edwards died eighteen years before the War of Independence, but the confidence that Americans were God's wilderness people bound to lead the world into the millennium burned brightly for several generations. Since then, the people of this country have been led astray and have in the process rejected the Christian's God. As a result, little hope of a millennium remains in post-America unless the system is Christianized once again. Before that occurs, however, the country could fall under the due judgment of God.

If the Son Shall Make You Free ...

Man has come a long way in some respects but only a short way in most matters of eternal worth. He has continually sought all that he desired apart from God.

The Christian church on the whole has been ineffective in its function of discipling all nations. Christianity has the key to life and freedom, and it's up to the Christian man to take charge of the cultural direction of the world.

All men without salvation are in servitude to sin and, therefore, in servitude to other men. Christ said, "If ... the Son shall make you free, you shall be free indeed" (John 8:36). The free man in Christ can confront the world without fear of the pain and sorrow that come from standing up for right and truth. Christian or non-Christian, we must not circumvent true freedom by giving ourselves over to "Totalitaria." Modern man with his faith in the ungodly institutionalized government in effect says, "Hail, Caesar! We who are about to die salute you!"

As men, we must assert that we are creatures of worth made in the image of God and not machines of the government. We must not submit to servitude because pleasure commends it or because fear demands it. In the words of the apostle Peter, "We must obey God rather than men" (Acts 5:29). We must stand with men like Patrick Henry, who when his young country was faced with giving in or fighting back met the challenge. On March 23, 1775, he rose from the pew in St. John's Episcopal Church in Richmond, Virginia, and said, "Is life so dear, or peace so sweet, as to be purchased at the price of chains and slavery? Forbid it, Almighty God! I know not what course others may take; but as for me ... give me liberty or give me death."

By God's Grace I have committed my life so wholly to Christ I say from the depths of my being that I've counted all but dung that I might win Christ as Lord of all, and as Patrick Henry said in the face of challenge, As for me ... give me liberty or give me death — Even then God empowers us to fight Satan and his army gaining the victory for the life He offers both here and me eternally hereafter —

D. Smitz

Notes

Prologue

1. James C. Hefley, *America: One Nation Under God* (Wheaton, IL: Victor Books, 1975), pp. 10–11.
2. Ibid., p. 11.
3. *Zorach* v. *Clauson*, 343 U.S. 306, 313 (1952).
4. Hefley, *America*, p. 17.
5. Ibid.
6. Edwin Scott Gaustad, *Historical Atlas of Religion in America* (New York and Evanston: Harper & Row, 1962), p. 4.
7. Ibid.
8. Hefley, *America*, p. 42.
9. Rousas John Rushdoony, *The Nature of the American System* (Nutley, NJ: Craig Press, 1965), p. 4.
10. Warren Chase, *The Life-Line of the Lone One; or, Autobiography of Warren Chase* (Boston: Colby & Rich, 1881), p. 23.
11. Rushdoony, *American System*, p. 4.
12. James W. Sire, *The Universe Next Door* (Downers Grove, IL: Inter-Varsity Press, 1976), p. 49. This work is an excellent discussion of deism as well as various other world views.
13. Ibid.
14. John Warwick Montgomery, *The Shaping of America* (Minneapolis: Bethany Fellowship, 1976), p. 56.
15. Hefley, *America*, p. 79.
16. Ibid.
17. Rousas John Rushdoony, *This Independent Republic* (Nutley, NJ: Craig Press, 1973), p. 6.
18. See chapter four for a more detailed examination of Jefferson's Unitarian faith.
19. Winthrop S. Hudson, *Religion in America*, 2d ed. (New York: Charles Scribner's Sons, 1973), pp. 95, 131–32.
20. For a more detailed discussion of Tocqueville's observations, see the last section of chapter two.
21. Hudson, *Religion in America*, p. 102.

22. C. Gregg Singer, *A Theological Interpretation of American History* (Nutley, NJ: Craig Press, 1969), p. 44.
23. Ibid., p. 42.
24. Ibid.
25. Ibid., p. 44.
26. Ibid., pp. 44–45.
27. Hudson, *Religion in America*, p. 94.
28. Montgomery, *Shaping of America*, p. 65.
29. Rushdoony, *American System*, p. 2.
30. Ibid., p. 3.
31. Singer, *A Theological Interpretation*, pp. 284–85.

Chapter 1

1. As quoted by Julius Fast, *The Beatles: The Real Story* (New York: Berkeley Medallion Books, 1968), p. 163.
2. Ibid., p. 165.
3. Ibid., p. 166.
4. Ibid.
5. R. J. Rushdoony, *Freud* (Nutley, NJ: Presbyterian & Reformed Publishing Co., 1975), p. 21.
6. Sigmund Freud, *The Future of an Illusion* (Garden City, NY: Anchor Books, 1964), p. 69.
7. Ibid., p. 59.
8. Ibid., p. 48.
9. As quoted by Rushdoony, *Freud*, pp. 37–38.
10. Walter Goodman, *The Committee* (New York: Farrar, Straus, 1968), p. 335.
11. *Time*, June 6, 1969, p. 88.
12. Ibid.
13. *Time*, December 10, 1965, p. 96.
14. B. F. Skinner, *Beyond Freedom and Dignity* (New York: Alfred A. Knopf, 1971), p. 33.
15. Ibid.
16. *Los Angeles Times*, March 13, 1976, p. 21.
17. Ibid.
18. Ibid.
19. Ibid.
20. Ibid.
21. *Los Angeles Times*, June 19, 1976, p. 29.
22. Ibid.
23. Ibid.
24. *Corpus Christi Caller*, April 29, 1975.
25. Ibid.
26. Ibid.
27. Ibid.

28. Bob Dylan, *It's Alright, Ma, I'm Only Bleeding* (New York: M. Witmark & Sons, 1965).
29. Wilmot Robertson, *The Dispossessed Majority* (Cape Canaveral, FL: Howard Allen, 1973), p. 264.
30. Ibid.
31. Ibid., p. 265.
32. Introductory note by R. J. Rushdoony, in Gary North, *Marx's Religion of Revolution: The Doctrine of Creative Destruction* (Nutley, NJ: Craig Press, 1968), p. 9.
33. Ibid.
34. Supreme Court Justice Hugo Black grudgingly acknowledges this fact in the New York prayer case—*Engel* v. *Vitale,* 370 U.S. 421, 427-28 (1962): "Indeed, as late as the time of the Revolutionary War, there were established churches in at least eight of the thirteen former colonies and established religions in at least four of the other five."
35. Francis A. Schaeffer, *The God Who Is There* (Downers Grove, IL: Inter-Varsity Press, 1968), p. 179.
36. Francis A. Schaeffer, *Back to Freedom and Dignity* (Downers Grove, IL: Inter-Varsity Press, 1972), p. 10.
37. *Los Angeles Times,* April 3, 1976.
38. Schaeffer, *Freedom and Dignity,* p. 46.

Chapter 2

1. Barry Goldwater, *The Coming Break-Point* (New York: Macmillan, 1976), p. 7.
2. *Time,* March 1, 1976, p. 59.
3. Goldwater, *Break-Point,* p. 3.
4. Edward S. Corwin, "The 'Higher Law' Background of American Constitutional Law," *Harvard Law Review* 62 (1928): 149, 150.
5. John Bach McMaster, *The Political Depravity of the Founding Fathers* (New York: Noonday Press, 1964), p. 112.
6. Frank Donovan, *Mr. Madison's Constitution* (New York: Dodd, Mead, 1965), p. 2.
7. Robert Allen Rutland, *The Birth of the Bill of Rights, 1776-1791* (Chapel Hill: University of North Carolina Press, 1955), pp. 170, 172.
8. Corwin, "American Constitutional Law," p. 150.
9. Ibid.
10. Ibid., p. 151.
11. Rus Walton, *One Nation Under God* (Old Tappan, NJ: Fleming H. Revell, 1975), p. 21.
12. Saul K. Padover, *The World of the Founding Fathers* (New York: Thomas Yoseloff, 1960), p. 315.
13. Amaury de Riencourt, *The Coming Caesars* (New York: Coward-McCann, 1957), p. 70.

14. Morris D. Forkosch, *Constitutional Law* (Mineola, NY: Foundation Press, 1969), p. 3.
15. James MacGregor Burns and J. W. Peltason, *Government by the People*, 3d ed. (Englewood Cliffs, NJ: Prentice-Hall, 1972), p. 29.
16. Ibid., p. 31.
17. James Charles Cooper, *The Recovery of America* (Philadelphia: Westminster Press, 1973), p. 161.
18. Burns and Peltason, *Government by the People*, p. 31.
19. Ibid.
20. Ibid.
21. Ibid., p. 32.
22. Peter Lowenberg, "The Vested Vision of Alexander Hamilton," *Los Angeles Times*, July 25, 1976, Book Review, p. 4.
23. Ibid.
24. John Silber, "A Few Words in Praise of Elitism," *Los Angeles Times*, July 14, 1976, p. 5.
25. Riencourt, *Coming Caesars*, p. 119.
26. Alexis de Tocqueville, *Democracy in America* (Garden City, NY: Doubleday, 1969), p. 267.
27. Lord Percy of Newcastle, *The Heresy of Democracy* (Chicago: Henry Regnery, 1955), p. 12.
28. Riencourt, *Coming Caesars*, p. 73.
29. Corwin, "American Constitutional Law," p. 152.
30. Ibid.
31. Riencourt, *Coming Caesars*, p. 73.
32. Ibid.
33. Erik von Kuehnelt-Leddihn, *Leftism: From de Sade and Marx to Hitler and Marcuse* (New Rochelle, NY: Arlington House, 1974), p. 48.
34. Ibid.
35. Ibid., p. 454.
36. Lord Percy, *Heresy*, p. 26.
37. Will and Ariel Durant, *Rousseau and Revolution* (New York: Simon & Schuster, 1967), p. 172.
38. Lord Percy, *Heresy*, p. 28.
39. Ibid.
40. *Los Angeles Times*, July 17, 1976, p. 25.
41. Ibid.
42. Lord Percy, *Heresy*, p. 11.
43. Kuehnelt-Leddihn, *Leftism*, p. 24.
44. Ibid.
45. Lord Percy, *Heresy*, p. 30.
46. Ibid.

47. Kuehnelt-Leddihn, *Leftism,* p. 26.
48. Lord Percy, *Heresy,* p. 31.
49. Jacques Ellul, *The Political Illusion* (New York: Vintage Books, 1972), p. 10.
50. John Lennon and Paul McCartney, *Back in the U.S.S.R.* (Apple Records, BMI).
51. Crane Brinston, John B. Christopher, and Robert Lee Wolff, *A History of Civilization* (Englewood Cliffs, NJ: Prentice-Hall, 1960), vol. 2, p. 460.
52. Ibid.
53. John Warwick Montgomery, *The Law Above the Law* (Minneapolis: Dimension Books, 1975), p. 11.
54. Brinston, et al., *Civilization,* p. 460.
55. Ibid.
56. *Marbury* v. *Madison,* I Cranch 137 (1803).
57. Jacques Ellul, *The Theological Foundation of Law* (New York: Seabury Press, 1969), p. 18.
58. Montgomery, *Law,* p. 11.
59. Padover, *Founding Fathers,* p. 298.
60. Ibid.
61. Ibid.
62. Silber, "Elitism," p. 5.
63. Ibid.
64. Ibid.
65. Ibid.
66. Riencourt, *Coming Caesars,* p. 286.
67. *Los Angeles Times,* July 17, 1976, p. 25.
68. Tocqueville, *Democracy,* p. 291.
69. Billy Graham, *Our Bicentennial: America at the Crossroads* (Minneapolis: Billy Graham Evangelistic Association, 1976), p. 7.
70. Ibid.
71. Ibid., p. 12.
72. Tocqueville, *Democracy,* p. 300.

Chapter 3

1. Richard C. Cortner and Clifford M. Lytle, *Modern Constitutional Law* (New York: Collier-MacMillan, 1971), p. 33.
2. Amaury de Riencourt, *The Coming Caesars* (New York: Coward-McCann, 1957), p. 164.
3. Ibid., pp. 165–66.
4. Carl Becker, *The Declaration of Independence* (New York: Alfred A. Knopf, 1942), pp. 241–42.

5. Lewis Perry, *Radical Abolition: Anarchy and the Government of God in Antislavery Thought* (Ithaca, NY: Cornell University Press, 1973), p. 17.
6. Ibid., p. 15.
7. Eugene H. Methvin, *The Rise of Radicalism* (New Rochelle, NY: Arlington House, 1973), p. 20.
8. *The Federalist Papers* (New York: Mentor Books, 1961), p. 181.
9. C. Gregg Singer, *A Theological Interpretation of American History* (Nutley, NJ: Craig Press, 1969), p. 5.
10. Becker, *Declaration*, p. 241–42.
11. R. J. Rushdoony, *The Nature of the American System* (Nutley, NJ: Craig Press, 1965), p. 49.
12. Edmund Wilson, *Patriotic Gore* (New York: Oxford University Press, 1962), p. 95.
13. Singer, *Theological Interpretation*, p. 84.
14. Riencourt, *Coming Caesars*, p. 172.
15. Ibid.
16. Ibid.
17. Ibid.
18. Ibid.
19. Ibid.
20. Bob Dylan, *Only a Pawn in Their Game* (New York: M. Witmark & Sons, 1963).
21. Walter J. Suthon, Jr., "The Dubious Origin of the Fourteenth Amendment," *Tulane Law Review* 28 (1953): 22, 30.
22. Stewart C. Easton, *A Brief History of the Western World* (New York: Barnes & Noble, 1962), pp. 328–29.
23. *Congressional Globe,* 39th Congress, 2d sess., Gart 3, 1644 (1867).
24. W. E. Woodward, *A New American History* (New York: Farrar & Rinehart, 1936), p. 634.
25. Ibid., p. 597.
26. Ibid.
27. Riencourt, *Coming Caesars,* p. 173.
28. Ibid.
29. Ibid.
30. Ibid., p. 174.
31. Ibid., p. 179.
32. Gordon Lightfoot, "Too Late for Prayin' " (Toronto: Moose Music, CAPAC, 1973).
33. Bernard Schwartz, *Statutory History of the United States: Part 1* (New York: Chelsea House, 1970), p. 181.
34. *Barron v. Baltimore,* 7 Peters 243 (1833).

35. Schwartz, *Statutory History*, p. 268.
36. Ibid., pp. 194, 248.
37. Ibid., p. 301.
38. Ibid., p. 306.
39. Schwartz, *Statutory History*, p. 334.
40. *The Slaughterhouse Cases*, 16 Wall 36 (1873).
41. Gerald Gunther and Noel T. Dowling, *Cases and Materials on Constitutional Law* (New York: Foundation Press, 1970), p. 804.
42. *Adamson* v. *California*, 332 U.S. 46 (1947).
43. John Denton Carter, *The Warren Court and the Constitution* (Gretna, LA: Pelican, 1973), p. 70.

Chapter 4

1. Dumas Malone, *Jefferson and His Time: Jefferson as President* (Boston: Little, Brown & Co., 1970), vol. 4, p. 190.
2. Fawn M. Brodie, *Thomas Jefferson: An Intimate History* (New York: W. W. Norton, 1974), p. 370.
3. Ibid., p. 372.
4. Ibid., p. 373.
5. Saul K. Padover, ed., *The World of the Founding Fathers* (New York and London: Thomas Yoseloff, 1960), p. 317. Quoted from a letter by Jefferson to Benjamin Waterhouse from Monticello, dated June 26, 1822, and printed in full in this excellent collection of early American writings.
6. Ibid.
7. Ibid.
8. *Engel* v. *Vitale*, 370 U.S. 421 (1962), *Prayer; School District of Abington Township, Pa.* v. *Schempp*, 374 U.S. 203 (1963), *Bible reading*.
9. *Everson* v. *Board of Education*, 330 U.S. 1, 17 (1947).
10. Saul K. Padover, ed., *The Complete Jefferson* (New York: Duell, Sloan & Pearce, 1943), pp. 518–19.
11. Edward S. Corwin, *American Constitutional History* (New York, Evanston, and London: Harper Torchbooks, 1965), p. 205.
12. Ibid.
13. Ibid., p. 206.
14. 3 Elliott, *The Debates of the Several State Conventions on the Adoption of the Federal Constitution*, 330 (2d ed., 1836).
15. *Reynolds* v. *U.S.*, 98 U.S. 145, 164 (1879).
16. Bob Dylan, *Another Side of Bob Dylan* (Bob Dylan, 1964).
17. As quoted by R. J. Rushdoony, *This Independent Republic* (Nutley, NJ: Craig Press, 1973), p. 37.

18. Wilmot Robertson, *The Dispossessed Majority* (Cape Canaveral, FL: Howard Allen, 1973), p. 252.
19. Corwin, *Constitutional History*, p. 205–6.

Chapter 5

1. *Reynolds* v. *U.S.*, 98 U.S. 145 (1878).
2. Ibid., 161.
3. Ibid., 166.
4. Ibid., 167.
5. R. J. Rushdoony, "The State as an Establishment of Religion" (an address given at Notre Dame School of Law, April 24, 1976), p. 4.
6. Jacques Ellul, *The Theological Foundation of Law* (New York: Seabury Press, 1960), p. 18.
7. Ibid.
8. *Cantwell* v. *Connecticut*, 310 U.S. 296 (1940).
9. *McCollum* v. *Board of Education*, 333 U.S. 203 (1948).
10. *Engel* v. *Vitale*, 370 U.S. 421, 422 (1962).
11. Ibid., 425.
12. Ibid.
13. Ernest J. Brown, "Quis Custodiet Ipsos Custodes?—The School Prayer Cases," in *Supreme Court Review* (Chicago: University of Chicago Press, 1963), p. 8.
14. Ibid., p. 436.
15. Saul K. Padover, *The Complete Madison* (New York: Harper & Brothers, 1953), p. 19.
16. I Annals of Congress, p. 759 (1789).
17. Ibid., pp. 783–84.
18. *Engel*, 431.
19. J. Marcellus Kik, *The Supreme Court and Prayer in the Public Schools* (Philadelphia: Presbyterian & Reformed Publishing Co., 1963), p. 7. This work is an excellent examination of the problem.
20. *Engel*, 425.
21. Barrington Moore, Jr., *Social Origins of Dictatorship and Democracy* (Boston: Beacon Press, 1966), p. 413.
22. *Engel*, 426.
23. Kik, *Prayer in the Public Schools*, p. 17.
24. Ibid.
25. Ibid., p. 34.
26. *Engel*, 430.
27. Ibid., 435.
28. Kik, *Prayer in the Public Schools*, p. 11.

29. Ibid.
30. *Engel*, 438.
31. Kik, *Prayer in the Public Schools*, p. 13.
32. *De Spain* v. *De Kalb County Community School District*, 384 F. 2d 836 (1967).
33. *Engel*, 437.
34. Ibid., 445.

Chapter 6

1. *School District of Abington Township* v. *Schempp* and *Murray* v. *Curlett*, 374 U.S. 203 (1963). Both cases were decided at once since both involved the same issues.
2. Alpheus Thomas Mason, *The Supreme Court from Taft to Warren* (New York: W. W. Norton, 1958), p. 29.
3. Ernest J. Brown, "Quis Custodiet Ipsos Custodes?—The School Prayer Cases," in *Supreme Court Review* (Chicago: University of Chicago Press, 1963), p. 4.
4. *Schempp*, 206, 211.
5. Walter R. Martin, *The Kingdom of the Cults* (Minneapolis: Bethany Fellowship, 1965), p. 425.
6. Ibid., p. 424.
7. *Schempp*, 205.
8. Ibid.
9. Ibid., 226.
10. Edward S. Corwin, *American Constitutional History* (New York: Harper Torchbooks, 1965), p. 205.
11. C. Gregg Singer, *The Theological Interpretation of American History* (Nutley, NJ: Craig Press, 1969), p. 133.
12. *Zorach* v. *Clauson*, 343 U.S. 306, 313 (1952).
13. Ibid.
14. *Walz* v. *Tax Commission of the City of New York*, 397 U.S. 664, 669 (1970).
15. *McCollum* v. *Board of Education*, 333 U.S. 203 (1948).
16. *Walz*, 670.
17. Ibid.
18. *Schempp*, 214.
19. "School Prayer and the Becker Amendment " *Georgetown Law Journal* 53 (1964): 192, 195.
20. *The Gospel Truth* 16, no. 8 (July 1976).
21. As quoted by Brown, *School Prayer Cases*, p. 14.
22. *Schempp*, 313.

23. Address given at 33rd Annual Convention of National Religious Broadcasters Convention, February 22–25, 1976, Washington, DC.

Chapter 7

1. H. W. Koch, *Hitler Youth: The Duped Generation* (New York: Ballantine Books, 1972), p. 23.
2. Ibid., p. 10.
3. Ibid., p. 116.
4. Jerry Rubin, *Do It!* (New York: Ballantine Books, 1970), p. 256.
5. *Los Angeles Times,* June 21, 1976, p. 1.
6. *National Observer,* June 12, 1976.
7. Ibid., p. 19.
8. *Time Magazine,* June 14, 1976, p. 49.
9. Ibid.
10. Ibid.
11. *National Observer,* June 12, 1976, p. 19.
12. Edward S. Corwin, *American Constitutional Law* (New York: Harper Torchbooks, 1964), p. 197.
13. J. Marcellus Kik, *The Supreme Court and Prayer in the Public School* (Philadelphia: Presbyterian & Reformed Publishing Co., 1963), p. 28.
14. For an excellent examination of this problem, see R. J. Rushdoony, *Intellectual Schizophrenia* (Philadelphia: Presbyterian & Reformed Publishing Co., 1961).
15. Kik, *Prayer in the Public Schools,* p. 30.
16. Ibid., p. 31.
17. Ibid.
18. *The Gospel Truth* 16, no. 4 (1976): 3.
19. Albert Rosenfeld, *The Second Genesis: The Coming Control of Life* (New York: Vintage Books, 1975), pp. 123ff.
20. *School District of Abington Township, Pa. v. Schempp,* 374 U.S. 203, 294 (1963).
21. Ibid., 306.
22. Ibid., 225.
23. *Christ for the Nations* 29, no. 1 (1976): 14.
24. Ibid.
25. *Los Angeles Times,* July 14, 1976, p. 5.
26. Ibid.
27. Ibid.
28. *Christ for the Nations* 29, no. 1 (1976): 14.
29. Ibid.
30. *Los Angeles Times,* July 14, 1976, p. 5.

31. *Newsweek,* December 8, 1975.
32. *Los Angeles Times,* April 3, 1976.
33. Ibid.
34. *McGowan* v. *Maryland,* 366 U.S. 420, 461 (1961).
35. As reported in "Constitutional Law—Religious Exercises in the Public Schools," *Arkansas Law Review* 20 (1967): 320, 340. This is an excellent discussion on the religious issue in the public schools.
36. Ibid., p. 341.
37. *Reed* v. *Van Hoven,* 237 F. Supp. 48, 53 (W. D. Mich. 1965).
38. Paul Simon, *Kodachrome* (Charing Music, BMI, 1973).
39. Koch, *Hitler Youth,* p. 158.

Chapter 8

1. *Los Angeles Times,* April 30, 1976, pt. 3.
2. *Gillette* v. *U.S.,* 401 U.S. 437, 463 (1971).
3. R. J. Rushdoony, *The Nature of the American System* (Nutley, NJ: Craig Press, 1965), p. 45.
4. Ibid.
5. Erik von Kuehnelt-Leddihn, *Leftism: From de Sade and Marx to Hitler and Marcuse* (New Rochelle, NY: Arlington House, 1974), p. 427.
6. Rushdoony, *American System,* p. 56.
7. *American Mercury* 89, no. 430 (1959): 136–38.
8. *Independent Record* (Thermopolis, WY), January 22, 1976.
9. Earl W. Kintner, *An Antitrust Primer* (New York: Macmillan, 1964), preface.

Chapter 9

1. Alvin Toffler, *Future Shock* (New York: Random House, 1970).
2. Fyodor Dostoevsky, *The Brothers Karamazov* (New York: Bantam Books, 1970).
3. Ibid., pp. 297–319.
4. Ibid., p. 304.
5. Ibid., p. 305.
6 Aldous Huxley, *Brave New World and Brave New World Revisited* (New York: Harper & Row, 1960), foreword.
7. Alexis de Tocqueville, *Democracy in America* (Garden City, NY: Anchor Books, 1960), p. 691.
8. *Time,* July 19, 1976, p. 35.
9. B. F. Skinner, *Beyond Freedom and Dignity* (New York: Alfred A Knopf, 1971) p. 34.

10. Ibid.
11. Ibid., p. 40.
12. Dostoevsky, *Brothers Karamazov*, p. 307.
13. Jacques Ellul, *The Political Illusion* (New York: Vintage Books, 1972).
14. Aleksandr Solzhenitsyn, "Gulag Survivor Indicts Western 'Freedoms,' " *Los Angeles Times*, June 13, 1976, p. 1.
15. Ibid.
16. Daniel P. Mannix, *Those About to Die* (New York: Ballantine Books, 1958), p. 27.
17. Pierre Grimal, *The Civilization of Rome* (New York: Simon & Schuster, 1963), pp. 332, 456.
18. Ethelbert Stauffer, *Christ and the Caesars* (Philadelphia: Westminster Press, 1955), p. 86.
19. *Los Angeles Times*, June 11, 1976, p. 3.
20. Ibid.
21. Dostoevsky, *Brothers Karamazov*, p. 307.
22. Ibid., p. 308.
23. Ellul, *Political Illusion*, p. 61.
24. Dostoevsky, *Brothers Karamazov*, p. 308.
25. Leonard Cohen, "Story of Isaac" (Stranger Music, BMI).
26. Stauffer, *Christ and the Caesars*, p. 283.
27. Ibid.
28. *New York Times*, June 26, 1976, p. 1.
29. *Los Angeles Times*, June 26, 1976, p. 14.
30. Ibid.
31. Ibid.
32. *The State of Ohio* v. *Whisner*, 47 Ohio St. 2d. 181 (1976).
33. Rexford G. Tugwell, *The Emerging Constitution* (New York: Harper & Row, 1974).
34. Ibid., p. 596.
35. Ibid.
36. Ernest Conine, "Socialism: America's *Real* Revolution," *Los Angeles Times*, July 9, 1976, p. 5.
37. Richard N. Goodwin, *The American Condition* (New York: Doubleday, 1974), p. 15.
38. Tugwell, *Emerging Constitution*, p. 597.
39. Manés Sperber, "I Am God! Do You Hear—God! (For a Minute)," *New York Times*, June 19, 1976.
40. Tugwell, *Emerging Constitution*, p. 620.
41. Roland Huntford, *The New Totalitarians* (New York: Stein & Day, 1972), p. 7.
42. Huxley, *Brave New World*, foreword.

43. Albert Rosenfeld, *The Second Genesis: The Coming Control of Life* (New York: Vintage Books, 1975), pp. 23–24.
44. Huntford, *New Totalitarians*, p. 9.
45. Huxley, *Brave New World*, foreword.
46. Rosenfeld, *Second Genesis*, p. 297.
47. Ibid.
48. Ibid.
49. Ibid., p. 298.
50. Ibid.
51. Ibid.
52. Ibid., p. 299.
53. Schaeffer, *Back to Freedom and Dignity* (Downers Grove, IL: Inter-Varsity Press, 1972), p. 25.
54. Ibid.
55. Huntford, *New Totalitarians*, p. 11.
56. William Irwin Thompson, " 'What's Past Is Prologue.' The Past—What's That?" *New York Times*, June 10, 1976, p. 37.
57. Ibid.
58. John Silber, "A Few Words in Praise of Elitism," *Los Angeles Times*, July 14, 1976, p. 5.
59. Huntford, *New Totalitarians*, p. 11.
60. Ibid.
61. *Los Angeles Times*, June 1, 1976.
62. *Los Angeles Times*, June 26, 1976, p. 24.
63. Hal Lindsey, *The Terminal Generation* (Old Tappan, NJ: Fleming H. Revell, 1976).
64. John Warwick Montgomery, *The Shaping of America* (Minneapolis: Bethany Fellowship, 1976), pp. 122–23.

Select Bibliography

Barker, Lucius J., and Barker, Twiley W., Jr. *Civil Liberties and the Constitution*. Englewood Cliffs, NJ: Prentice-Hall, 1970.

Bartholomew, Paul C. *Ruling American Constitutional Law*. Totowa, NJ: Littlefield, Adams & Co., 1970.

Bastiat, Frederic. *The Law*. Irvington-on-Hudson, NY: Foundation for Economic Education, 1968.

Becker, Carl. *The Declaration of Independence*. New York: Alfred A. Knopf, 1942.

Bob Dylan Song Book. New York: M. Witmark & Sons.

Boettner, Loraine. *The Reformed Doctrine of Predestination*. Philadelphia: Presbyterian & Reformed, 1963.

Bradley, Harold Whitman. *The United States 1492–1877*. New York: Charles Scribner's Sons, 1972.

Brinston, Crane; Christopher, John; and Wolff, Robert Lee. *A History of Civilization*. Englewood Cliffs, NJ: Prentice-Hall, 1960.

Brodie, Fawn M. *Thomas Jefferson: An Intimate History*. New York: W. W. Norton, 1974.

Brown, Ernest J. "Quis Custodiet Ipsos Custodes?—The School Prayer Cases." *Supreme Court Review*. Chicago: University of Chicago Press, 1963.

Burke, Edmund, and Paine, Thomas. *Reflections on the Revolution and the Rights of Man*. Garden City, NY: Dolphin Books, 1961.

Burns, James MacGregor, and Peltason, J. W. *Government by the People*. 3d ed. Englewood Cliffs, NJ: Prentice-Hall, 1972.

Calvin, John. *Calvin's Institutes*. MacDill AFB, FL: MacDonald Publishing Co.

Carter, John Denton. *The Warren Court and the Constitution*. Gretna, LA: Pelican, 1973.

Chase, Warren. *The Life-Line of the Lone One; or, Autobiography of Warren Chase*. Boston: Colby & Rich, 1881.

Conlan, John B. *Let Freedom Ring*. Oklahoma City: Southwest Radio Church, 1976.

"Constitutional Law—Religious Exercises in the Public Schools." *Arkansas Law Review* 20 (1967).

Cooke, Alistair. *Alistair Cooke's America*. New York: Alfred A. Knopf, 1973.

Cooke, Edward F. *A Detailed Analysis of the Constitution*. Totowa, NJ: Littlefield, Adams & Co., 1974.

Cooke, Jacob C., ed. *The Federalist*. Middletown, CT: Wesleyan University Press, 1975.

Cooper, James Charles. *The Recovery of America*. Philadelphia: Westminster Press, 1973.

Cortner, Richard C., and Lytle, Clifford M. *Modern Constitutional Law*. New York: Collier-MacMillan, 1971.

Corwin, Edward S. *American Constitutional History*. New York, Evanston, and London: Harper Torchbooks, 1965.

————. *The Constitution and What It Means Today*. Revised by Harold W. Chase and Craig R. Ducat. 13th ed. Princeton, NJ: Princeton University Press, 1975.

————. "The 'Higher Law' Background of American Constitutional Law." *Harvard Law Review* 62 (1928).

Davies, Hunter. *The Beatles: The Authorized Biography*. New York: McGraw-Hill, 1968.

Dewey, John. *A Common Faith*. New Haven: Yale University Press, 1934.

Donovan, Frank. *Mr. Madison's Constitution*. New York: Dodd, Mead, 1965.

Dostoevsky, Fyodor. *The Brothers Karamazov*. New York: Bantam Books, 1970.

Drucker, Peter F. *The Unseen Revolution*. New York: Harper & Row, 1976.

Durant, Will and Ariel. *The Age of Napoleon*. New York: Simon & Schuster, 1975.

————. *Rousseau and Revolution*. New York: Simon & Schuster, 1967.

Easton, Stewart C. *A Brief History of the Western World*. New York: Barnes & Noble, 1962.

3 Elliot. *The Debates of the Several State Conventions of the Adoption of the Federal Constitution*. 2d ed. 1836.

Ellul, Jacques. *The Political Illusion*. New York: Vintage Press, 1972.

————. *The Theological Foundation of Law*. New York: Seabury Press, 1969.

Fast, Julius. *The Beatles: The Real Story*. New York: Berkeley Medallion Books, 1968.

Ferrero, Guglielmo, and Barbagallo, Corrado. *A Short History of Rome*. 2 vols. New York: Knickerbocker Press, 1919.

Foner, Eric. *Tom Paine and Revolutionary America*. New York: Oxford University Press, 1976.

Foner, Phillip S., ed. *Basic Writings of Thomas Jefferson*. Garden City, NY: Halcyon House, 1950.

Forkosch, Morris D. *Constitutional Law*. Mineola, NY: Foundation Press, 1969.

Freeman, David Hugh. *A Philosophical Study of Religion*. Nutley, NJ: Craig Press, 1964.

Freud, Sigmund. *Civilization and Its Discontents*. New York: Doubleday, 1958.

_____. *The Future of an Illusion*. Garden City, NY: Anchor Books, 1964.

_____. *Moses and Monotheism*. New York: Alfred A. Knopf, 1949.

Friedman, Lawrence M. *A History of American Law*. New York: Simon & Schuster, 1973.

Gaustad, Edwin Scott. *Historical Atlas of Religion in America*. New York: Harper & Row, 1962.

Gibbon, Edward. *The Decline and Fall of the Roman Empire*. 3 vols. New York: Washington Square Press, 1972.

Goldwater, Barry. *The Coming Break-Point*. New York: Macmillan, 1976.

Goodman, Walter. *The Committee*. New York: Farrar, Straus, 1968.

Goodwin, Richard N. *The American Condition*. New York: Doubleday, 1974.

Graham, Billy. *Our Bicentennial: America at the Crossroads*. Minneapolis: Billy Graham Evangelistic Association, 1976.

Grimal, Pierre. *The Civilization of Rome*. New York: Simon & Schuster, 1963.

Guinness, Os. *The Dust of Death*. Downers Grove, IL: Inter-Varsity Press, 1973.

_____. *Violence: A Study of Contemporary Attitudes*. Downers Grove, IL: Inter-Varsity Press, 1974.

Gunther, Gerald, and Dowling, Noel T. *Cases and Materials on Constitutional Law*. New York: Foundation Press, 1970.

Hall, Verna M. *Christian History of the Constitution of the United States of America*. Vols. 1, 2. San Francisco: American Constitution Press, 1961.

Hefley, James C. *America: One Nation Under God*. Wheaton, IL: Victor Books, 1975.

Hertz, Richard. *Chance and Symbol*. Chicago: University of Chicago Press, 1948.

Holmes, Oliver Wendell. *The Common Law*. Boston: Little, Brown & Co., 1938.

Howe, Mark DeWolfe. *Holmes-Laski Letters*. Cambridge: Harvard University Press, 1953.

Hudson, Winthrop S. *Religion in America*. New York: Charles Scribner's Sons, 1973.

Huntford, Roland. *The New Totalitarians.* New York: Stein & Day, 1972.

Huxley, Aldous. *Brave New World and Brave New World Revisited.* New York: Harper & Row, 1960.

Jackson, Robert H. *The Supreme Court in the American System of Government.* New York: Harper & Row, 1963.

Jones, R. Ben. *The French Revolution.* London: Minerva Press, 1967.

Kauper, Paul G. *Civil Liberties and the Constitution.* Ann Arbor: University of Michigan Press, 1966.

Kik, J. Marcellus. *The Supreme Court and Prayer in the Public Schools.* Philadelphia: Presbyterian & Reformed, 1963.

Kintner, Earl W. *An Antitrust Primer.* New York: Macmillan, 1964.

Koch, H. W. *Hitler Youth: The Duped Generation.* New York: Ballantine Books, 1972.

Koop, C. Everett. *The Right to Live; The Right to Die.* Wheaton, IL: Tyndale House, 1976.

Kuehnelt-Leddihn, Erik von. *Leftism: From de Sade and Marx to Hitler and Marcuse.* New Rochelle, NY: Arlington House, 1974.

Lewis, C. S. *The Abolition of Man.* New York: Macmillan, 1975.

Lindsey, Hal. *The Terminal Generation.* Old Tappan, NJ: Fleming H. Revell, 1976.

Locke, John. *On the Reasonableness of Christianity.* Chicago: Henry Regnery, 1965.

McDonald, Lawrence Patton. *We Hold These Truths.* Seal Beach, CA: '76 Press, 1976.

McDowell, Josh. *Evidence That Demands a Verdict.* Vol. 1. San Bernadino, CA: Campus Crusade for Christ, 1972.

McMaster. *The Political Depravity of the Founding Fathers.* New York: Noonday Press, 1964.

Malone, Dumas. *Jefferson and His Time: Jefferson as President.* Vol. 4. Boston: Little, Brown & Co., 1970.

Mannix, Daniel P. *Those About to Die.* New York: Ballantine Books, 1958.

Marshall, John. *The Life of George Washington.* Philadelphia: James Crissy, 1835.

Martin, Walter R. *The Kingdom of the Cults.* Minneapolis: Bethany Fellowship, 1965.

Mason, Alpheus Thomas. *The Supreme Court from Taft to Warren.* New York: W. W. Norton, 1958.

Meade, Robert Douthat. *Patrick Henry: Practical Revolutionary.* New York: J. B. Lippincott, 1969.

Methvin, Eugene H. *The Rise of Radicalism.* New Rochelle, NY: Arlington House, 1973.

Miller, Perry. *The Life of the Mind in America*. London: Victor Gallancz, 1966.

Monsma, Stephen V. *The Unraveling of America*. Downers Grove, IL: Inter-Varsity Press, 1974.

Montgomery, John Warwick. *The Law Above the Law*. Minneapolis: Dimension Books, 1975.

_____. *The Shaping of America*. Minneapolis: Bethany Fellowship, 1976.

Moore, Barrington, Jr. *Social Origins of Dictatorship and Democracy*. Boston: Beacon Press, 1966.

Morris, Desmond. *The Naked Ape*. New York: Dell, 1967.

Morris, Richard B. *Seven Who Shaped Our Destiny*. New York: Harper & Row, 1973.

Myrdal, Gunnar. *Beyond the Welfare State*. New York: Bantam Books, 1967.

North, Gary. *An Introduction to Christian Economics*. Nutley, NJ: Craig Press, 1974.

_____. *Marx's Religion of Revolution: The Doctrine of Creative Destruction*. Nutley, NJ: Craig Press, 1968.

Orwell, George. *Animal Farm*. New York: New American Library, 1963.

_____. *Nineteen Eighty-Four*. New York: Harcourt, Brace & World, 1949.

Padover, Saul K., ed. *The Complete Jefferson*. New York: Duell, Sloan & Pearce, 1943.

_____. *The Complete Madison*. New York: Harper & Brothers, 1953.

_____. *The World of the Founding Fathers*. New York: Thomas Yoseloff, 1960.

Percy of Newcastle, Lord. *The Heresy of Democracy*. Chicago: Henry Regnery, 1955.

Perry, Lewis. *Radical Abolition: Anarchy and the Government of God in Antislavery Thought*. Ithaca, NY: Cornell University Press, 1973.

Reich, Charles. *The Greening of America*. New York: Bantam, 1971.

Riencourt, Amaury de. *The Coming Caesars*. New York: Coward-McCann, 1957.

Robertson, Wilmot. *The Dispossessed Majority*. Cape Canaveral, FL: Howard Allen, 1973.

Rosenfeld, Albert. *The Second Genesis: The Coming Control of Life*. New York: Vintage Press, 1975.

Rowe, H. Edward. *Save America!* Old Tappan, NJ: Fleming H. Revell, 1976.

Rozwenc, Edwin C. *The Causes of the American Civil War*. Boston: D.C. Heath, 1961.

Rubin, Jerry. *Do It!* New York: Ballantine Books, 1970.

_____. *We Are Everywhere*. New York: Harper & Row, 1971.

Rushdoony, Rousas John. *Freud*. Presbyterian & Reformed, 1975.
———. *The Institutes of Biblical Law*. Nutley, NJ: Craig Press, 1973.
———. *Intellectual Schizophrenia*. Philadelphia: Presbyterian & Reformed, 1961.
———. *The Messianic Character of American Education*. Nutley, NJ: Craig Press, 1972.
———. *The Nature of the American System*. Nutley, NJ: Craig Press, 1965.
———. *The One and the Many*. Nutley, NJ: Craig Press, 1971.
———. *Politics of Guilt and Pity*. Nutley, NJ: Craig Press, 1970.
———. *The Politics of Pornography*. New Rochelle, NY: Arlington, House, 1974.
———. *This Independent Republic*. Nutley, NJ: Craig Press, 1973.
———. *The Word of Flux*. Fairfax, VA: Thoburn Press, 1975.
Russell, Francis. *Adams: An American Dynasty*. New York: American Heritage, 1976.
Rutland, Robert Allen. *The Birth of the Bill of Rights, 1776–1791*. Chapel Hill: University of North Carolina Press, 1955.
Scaduto, Anthony. *The Beatles*. New York: New American Library, 1968.
———. *Bob Dylan: An Intimate Biography*. New York: Castle Books, 1971.
Schaeffer, Francis A. *Back to Freedom and Dignity*. Downers Grove, IL: Inter-Varsity Press, 1972.
———. *Death in the City*. Downers Grove, IL: Inter-Varsity Press, 1973.
———. *Escape from Reason*. Downers Grove, IL: Inter-Varsity Press, 1968.
———. *The God Who Is There*. Downers Grove, IL: Inter-Varsity Press, 1968.
———. *He Is There and He Is Not Silent*. Wheaton, IL: Tyndale House, 1972.
"School Prayer and the Becker Amendment." *Georgetown Law Journal* 53 (1964).
Schwartz, Bernard. *Statutory History of the United States*. 2 vols. New York: Chelsea House, 1970.
Shaw, Peter. *The Character of John Adams*. Chapel Hill: University of North Carolina Press, 1976.
Sheperd, Billy. *The True Story of the Beatles*. New York: Bantam Books, 1964.
Singer, C. Gregg. *A Theological Interpretation of American History*. Nutley, NJ: Craig Press, 1969.
Sire, James W. *The Universe Next Door*. Downers Grove, IL: Inter-Varsity Press, 1976.

Skinner, B. F. *Beyond Freedom and Dignity*. New York: Alfred A. Knopf, 1971.

Solzhenitsyn, Aleksandr I. *The Gulag Archipelago Two*. New York: Harper & Row, 1975.

Stauffer, Ethelbert. *Christ and the Caesars*. Philadelphia: Westminster Press, 1955.

Suthon, Walter J., Jr. "The Dubious Origin of the Fourteenth Amendment." *Tulane Law Review* 28 (1953).

Swindler, William F. *Court and Constitution in the Twentieth Century*. 3 vols. Indianapolis and New York: Bobbs-Merrill, 1969.

Tatarkiewicz, Wladyslaw. *Nineteenth Century Philosophy*. Belmont, CA: Wadsworth, 1973.

Tocqueville, Alexis de. *Democracy in America*. Garden City, NY: Doubleday, 1969.

Toffler, Alvin. *The Eco-Spasm Report*. New York: Bantam Books, 1975.

_____. *Future Shock*. New York: Random House, 1970.

Tugwell, Rexford G. *The Emerging Constitution*. New York: Harper & Row, 1974.

Unger, Irwin, and Reimers, David, eds. *The Slavery Experience in the United States*. New York: Holt, Rinehart & Winston, 1970.

Van Til, Cornelius. *The Defense of the Faith*. Philadelphia: Presbyterian & Reformed, 1967.

Wahl, Jean. *A Short History of Existentialism*. New York: Philosophical Library, 1949.

Walton, Rus. *One Nation Under God*. Old Tappan, NJ: Fleming H. Revell, 1975.

Weizenbaum, Joseph. *Computer Power and Human Reason: From Judgment to Calculation*. San Francisco: W. H. Freeman, 1976.

Wells, H. G. *The Outline of History*. Garden City, NY: Doubleday, 1930.

White, G. Edward. *The American Judicial Tradition*. New York: Oxford University Press, 1976.

White, George Abbott, and Newman, Charles, eds. *Literature in Revolution*. New York: Holt, Rinehart & Winston, 1972.

Wilson, Edmund. *Patriotic Gore*. New York: Oxford University Press, 1962.

Woodward, W. E. *A New American History*. New York: Farrar & Rinehart, 1936.

Wormser, Rene A. *The Law*. New York: Simon & Schuster, 1949.

Index
Subjects and Names

Scripture